Above All Else

My Heart, My Responsibility

Jon Norman

Praise for *Above All Else*

In an age where intellect and reason rule the day—and information is everywhere—the heart still rules, whether we acknowledge it or not. Scripture is clear: What flows from the heart shapes the life. That's why this message matters. Jon writes with the rare blend of pastoral warmth and practical clarity, helping readers name what's happening beneath the surface and inviting them into realignment with God. These pages don't just offer insight; they aim at transformation—guiding you toward healing, freedom, and a restored inner life. Read it slowly, let it search you, and allow the Spirit to reform your heart from the inside out.

—Pastors Eric and Natalie Morris - Victory City Church,
Austin, Texas

Above All Else is a timely and heartfelt invitation to return to what matters most, the condition of our hearts before God. With honesty, wisdom, and deep pastoral care, this book gently challenges readers to slow down, let go of distractions, and allow Jesus to do His transforming work within. It is both convicting and encouraging, offering hope, freedom, and renewal for anyone longing for a deeper, more authentic walk with God.

—Coach Tom Mullins

The condition of our hearts shapes the direction of our lives, and Pastor Jon has a God-given ability to draw wisdom from Scripture and use it to help realign our inner worlds in a warm, funny, and practical way with real biblical depth.

This isn't just a book to read and shelve but a tried-and-tested trusted companion for the ongoing work of heart transformation.

—Pastors Dave and Abs Niblock - North Church, Leeds

Above All Else is more than a book. In its essence, it is the journal of the life of the author Jon Norman. He gives us a living diary of the day-to-day spiritual engagement of a leader who shares his lived experience with us. He has self-tested the content. What he shares is what he lives.

Priority matters. This is the book's central takeaway message that challenges every Christian. *Above All Else* frames the Christian's objective of living well in a turbulent world with its demands for the uncompromising guarding of our hearts as the essential source of not only spiritual but emotional and relational strength.

Based on Proverbs 4:23, Jon's book skillfully develops the practical message of the verse: how to protect the heart. Jon recognises that everything we do in our everyday lives—in our homes, workplaces, and relationships—flows from this cornerstone of spiritual power and authority. Whether you're committed in faith or simply curious, *Above All Else* is a thought-provoking and authentic call to examine what really comes first in our lives.

—Ken Costa - Spiritual father and Chairman of Emeritus of Alpha International and Dean of the Leadership College London

I feel very blessed to speak about the author, because I know him like no other—I'm his mum! Jon's steadfast faith, passion, and humour have been his hallmark over the years. Winning souls and cheering people on to stand in the truth of God's Word have been the passion of his life.

His heart is genuine—his heart is for Jesus—and he has a unique loving rawness in his way of communicating the gospel. I am thrilled he has written a book on God's heart and to encourage us all to protect our own hearts! I fully recommend you to read this book and allow God's heart to align with yours so we may grow together in the true grace of God.

—Gillian Norman - Mum

Pastor Jon is a special friend whom we have had the privilege of knowing for many years! He is a gifted communicator and has spoken to countless people all over the world. This book follows the same clear, practical, challenging style—it's full of biblical wisdom with a sprinkling of his unique sense of humour to keep it real! Buy this book, gift this book, and read this book. But most importantly act on the biblical truths that are within it, because everything we do flows from it!

—Mark and Sharon Hollinger, SOUL Church Elders

"Above all else, guard your heart." In many ways, this is a one-sentence autobiography of Solomon's life. In *Above All Else*, Pastor Jon Norman skillfully explores why your heart matters so deeply. He proven biblical wisdom and pastoral truth to help you guard your heart. As you read, our prayer is that God would do what Solomon could not—that God would guard your heart and bring strength, freedom, and transformation from the inside out.

—Steve and Rachel Mawston - Lifelong friends

In a world where the battle for our attention, minds and hearts is fiercer and more relentless than ever, the call of Proverbs 4:23 to guard your heart feels almost more important and relevant than it did during the reign of King Solomon nearly a thousand years before the birth of Christ.

We love this timely book from Jon Norman, because our hearts are the fulcrum upon which our lives and faith rest.

Above All Else is a book full of wisdom, honesty, and practical help that will help you understand more fully why our hearts matter, and how they are shaped by what we allow in.

If your heart is in need of some surgery, let *Above All Else* gently challenge you, encourage you, and get your heart realigned back with the heart of God which brings healing, freedom, and a life fulfilled.

—Simon and Derrina Thomas

Over the past several years, we've had the privilege to walk alongside you, Jon, as friends and as pastors. We are overjoyed to watch your heart for God, your love for people and your deep, abiding faith even through challenging seasons now be given as a testimony and an encouragement to others through the pages of *Above All Else*.

This book is going to inspire others to dig deep, to overcome challenges, to expand their perspectives and to have a fresh fire God's purpose, all while keeping their hearts pure and pliable and set part for His purpose.

Watching you live out the message of this book has inspired us and will strengthen countless others!

***—Pastors Joe and Lori Champion - Celebration Church,
Austin, Texas***

To my wife, Chantel, for your love and faith.

To my children, Miracle-Joy and Justice-Murray, my greatest joy.

To my parents, Gillian and Murray Norman, for the legacy you gave me.

To my SOUL Church family, this book is ours.

Contents

Foreword

By Pastor Rich Wilkerson Jr. – VOUS Church, Miami, Florida

In a world obsessed with the visible, the measurable, and the impressive, we are constantly tempted to evaluate life from the outside in. We celebrate external wins, chase external goals, and admire external success. But Scripture quietly reminds us that real success has always been an inside job.

The wisest man who ever lived wrote these words: "Above all else, guard your heart, for everything you do flows from it" (Proverbs 4:23).

Above all else.

Solomon wrote about relationships, parenting, money, friendship, discipline, wisdom, and leadership. Yet after addressing nearly every dimension of human life, he pauses and says above all of it, guard your heart.

Because everything flows from there.

I have learned this personally in my own life and leadership. There have been seasons where everything on the outside looked strong. The church was growing. Opportunities were increasing. The calendar was full. Yet internally, I could feel the warning signs of fatigue, distraction, and misplaced motivation. Nothing had "gone wrong," but something inside was drifting. And I realized how easy it is to manage what people see while neglecting what only God sees.

There is something deceptive about momentum.

When you have it, you assume you will always have it.

When you lose it, you assume you will never get it back.

Both are lies.

Momentum can be the most dangerous season of all, because you can be moving very fast without realizing you are no longer pedaling.

You forget that it was the quiet, unseen effort uphill that created the force now carrying you forward. The same disciplines, priorities, and attentiveness that built the momentum are the very things you slowly stop tending to once the motion feels automatic.

You are still moving, but you are no longer engaged.

And that is where drift begins.

That is why guarding the heart matters so deeply. Because you can have speed without health. Progress without presence. Growth without depth.

The tragedy is not losing momentum. The tragedy is mistaking momentum for maturity.

Solomon understood this long before we did. Above all else, guard your heart, because the heart is what keeps you pedaling when the road feels easy and when it feels uphill again.

We live in a time when many people break down but never stop to examine the engine. We are driven, ambitious, and full of plans, yet rarely do we pause to ask what is actually driving us. It is not wrong to dream. It is not wrong to be motivated. It is not wrong to pursue something meaningful. But it is foolish to neglect the condition of the heart that fuels it all.

Guarding your heart, then, is not passive. It is active. Intentional. Vigilant.

Most of us keep our money in a bank. Behind the screens and statements, there is a vault where the real currency is stored. Not everyone has access to that vault. Access is restricted. It is protected. It is guarded.

Imagine if we treated our hearts with the same care.

Not every voice deserves access. Not every situation deserves entry. Not every disappointment, headline, hurt, algorithm, or influence should be allowed to settle there.

The heart must be guarded because the heart is sacred. And because from it, life flows.

In these pages, Jon Norman invites us into this sacred work. With both beauty and practicality, he offers more than inspiration. He offers direction. He helps us consider how to protect the inner life so that our outer life can endure. He reminds us that talent is not enough, ambition is not enough, and success is not enough if the heart remains unattended.

Above All Else will help you cultivate the character, integrity, perseverance, and resilience required not only to start the journey, but to last in it.

Solomon gave us the command. Jon helps us live it.

And if you will take the time to apply what you read here, you may discover that the most important work you will ever do is not what the world sees, but what you carefully guard within.

By J.John – UK Evangelist

It has often been said that "the heart of the human problem is the problem of the human heart." And it's true. The heart—what we want, what we love, what we long for, what we secretly chase—sits at the very centre of every human life. Scratch beneath the surface of any decision, any direction, any devotion, and you will always find a heart at work.

In fact, I'd go further. Judging by this excellent book, my good friend Jon Norman would agree: The heart is not just a problem of our age—it is *the* problem of our age.

Look around the world today, both inside and outside the church, and you'll see a range of heart conditions everywhere. I would suggest there are three unhealthy ones that are alarmingly common and one healthy one that is, tragically, rare.

1. *The diluted heart*
   This is the heart with no fire in the belly. No burning desire. No holy ambition. No compelling "why."

2. *The distracted heart*
   These people are full of passion, drive, vision, and determination, but aimed at the wrong things, or at things of secondary importance.

3. *The divided heart*
   This is perhaps the most common condition of all. These people genuinely want many good things but those desires compete, collide, and constantly change. The heart is pulled in every direction and ends up going nowhere.

But then there is the fourth heart—the one we desperately need. The *dedicated heart*.

And that is precisely what this timely and immensely helpful book calls us towards.

A dedicated heart is one where God and His purposes are not merely included but enthroned. It is a full-strength heart. An undiluted heart. A focused heart. A heart captured by one great devotion and one overriding priority. Church leaders know this to be true: Give me ten people with dedicated hearts, and they will accomplish more than a hundred with hearts that are diluted, distracted, or divided.

The great verse that underpins everything this book teaches is Proverbs 4:23: "Above all else, guard your heart, for everything you do flows from it.

Above All Else is not just a book to read—it is one to wrestle with. Read it slowly. Read it prayerfully. Read it with an open heart. Underline it. Apply it. Live it. And may God use it to ignite hearts that beat with holy passion, fierce devotion, and an unshakeable commitment to Him—because when the heart is right, everything else follows.

Introduction

The title and underlying message of this book come from a single, powerful verse in the book of Proverbs:

Above all else, guard your heart, for everything you do flows from it.
(4:23)

These words were written by King Solomon, who lived around one thousand years before Jesus. Solomon became king of Israel as a teenager—young, inexperienced, and painfully aware of how out of his depth he was. (Anyone relate?)

One night, God appeared to Solomon in a dream and offered him anything he wanted. Imagine that moment. Unlimited possibility. No restrictions.

Solomon's response is recorded in 1 Kings 3. Instead of asking for wealth, power, influence, or success, he prayed:

> "I am like a little child who doesn't know his way around. And here I am in the midst of your own chosen people. . . . Give me an understanding heart so that I can govern your people well and know the difference between right and wrong."

Solomon could have asked for *anything,* but he asked for an understanding heart.

As a dad, husband, pastor, and chaplain, I've come to realise something sobering: If there is one thing with the power either to catapult me into my God-given destiny or quietly destroy it, it is my heart.

I have seen countless gifted leaders, strong marriages, meaningful friendships, and healthy relationships fall apart—not because of a lack of talent or calling, but because hearts were left unguarded.

This book is not written by someone who has his heart perfectly together. Quite the opposite. It is written by someone who has made mistakes, got it wrong in many of these areas, and yet has experienced the redeeming and healing power of Jesus firsthand.

Like Solomon, my desire is that we would begin to understand both the complexity *and* the beauty of the human heart. I truly believe life can be better, relationships healthier, and marriages stronger if we are willing to slow down and commit to examining and restoring our hearts with the help of the Holy Spirit.

Jesus said in John 10:10 that the enemy comes to steal, kill, and destroy. The enemy of our lives will always go after what can cause the most damage—and the heart is exactly that place. That is why, *above all else*, we must guard and understand our hearts.

This book is made up of ten chapters that are practical, applicable, and adaptable to your unique context. Our lives, our cultures, and our contexts may well look different, but the principles found in these pages remain the same.

My prayer for you as you read is that God would reveal, challenge, and transform your heart. Our hearts are always a work in progress. Just when we think we've got things together, something new can creep in. That's why this book isn't meant to be read once and shelved, but used as a resource you can return to whenever your heart needs attention.

Throughout these ten chapters, you'll notice three consistent patterns:

- **A Challenge** – Each chapter presents a specific challenge to apply.

- **A Question** – *Holy Spirit, what are You saying to me personally about this area of my heart, and how do You want me to respond?*

- **A Prayer** – A focused prayer invites God's peace and transformation into your life.

If you're reading this and you wouldn't yet call yourself a follower of Christ, I want to encourage you to keep going. There is so much here that you can apply to your life—and who knows, by the end of the journey you may find yourself asking deeper questions about faith, purpose, and eternity.

Seatbelts on. The plane is ready for takeoff, and remember: Your heart is your responsibility.

CHAPTER 1

The Incline of the Heart

Recently, I was on a much-needed treadmill run, and let me tell you: The treadmill is a terrible invention. Whoever came up with the idea of running in one place, staring at the same wall for half an hour, deserves to answer for their sins. At least outside, you can pretend you're running away from something. On a treadmill, you're basically a hamster with Spotify.

But as I was sweating it out, God gave me a simple word, two key verses from Psalm 119—the longest chapter in the Bible. It's a celebration of God's Word, widely assumed to be written by David. Listen to these two verses:

> I have inclined my heart to perform Your statutes forever, to the very end. I hate the double-minded, but I love Your law. (Psalm 119:112–113 NKJV)

Now, here's what struck me on that treadmill: I had it set on incline. And I discovered something profound: Recline is a lot easier than incline. Put the book down now and laugh at me—but how funny yet simple is that? It takes effort, sweat, calories, and energy to incline. It hurts! Staying in recline is comfortable. But staying in recline also means no progress, no reward, and no growth.

David said, "I have inclined my heart." Which means at some point, his heart must have been in recline—a negative posture, an unhelpful position. So he had to re-posture his heart the right way. And if David needed to do it, we do too. Because a lot of us go through life with our hearts reclined—comfortable, disengaged, not really pressing forward.

Let me give us three spiritual truths we can use to daily incline our hearts toward God:

1. **I recognise when my heart is in recline.**
   David said, "I have inclined my heart" (v. 112). Notice he didn't say, "God, You have inclined it for me." He took responsibility. Our heart is our responsibility. We can't always control the things that happen around us or even to us—but we are in charge of what happens inside of us.
   How many times have we heard someone say, "Oh, he stole my heart"? No, he didn't, sunshine. Nobody can break what we don't give them. The truth is, we hand people the keys to our heart, and then we blame them when they crash it into the wall. David knew better. He said, "I have inclined my heart." He owned it. And so must we.

2. **I redirect my heart when it drifts.**
   He said, "I have inclined my heart to perform Your statutes forever, to the very end" (112 NKJV). That's not a one-time action; it's a daily decision. Just like on the treadmill—you don't just hit "incline" once and then coast. You've got to keep walking, keep sweating, keep moving. Spiritually, it's the same. Our heart naturally drifts toward recline. It takes conscious redirection to bring it back.

   > When our heart is inclined toward God, our life moves in His direction.

3. **I resist the double-minded life.**
   David follows up with verse 113 (NKJV): "I hate the double-minded, but I love Your law." Double-mindedness is exhausting. It's like trying to run on a treadmill while also scrolling Instagram. One foot in, one foot out. No wonder we feel spiritually scattered. David says, "I love Your law." He found focus by fixing his heart on God's Word.

Here's the big idea: A heart on incline doesn't happen by accident. It takes recognition, redirection, and resistance. It takes effort. It hurts sometimes. But the reward is worth it. Because when our heart is inclined toward God, our life moves in His direction.

I Recognise When My Heart's in Recline

It can happen in a moment. You're doing fine, walking tall, worship playlist on, feeling like you could take on the world. Then *boom*—something hits and suddenly your heart is reclined. Maybe it's an email that makes your blood pressure spike. Maybe it's a phone call you didn't want to take. Maybe it's a driver cutting you off on the highway. Or maybe it's just a memory from years ago that pops into your head at the worst possible time. One second we're upright, the next we're flat.

Psalm 119:112 says: "I have inclined my heart to perform Your statutes forever, to the very end." Our hearts don't incline by default. They recline by default! Recline is Netflix, snacks, and "one more episode." Recline is easy. Incline takes effort. Incline takes energy. Incline takes sweat.

But here's the danger: When we stay in recline for too long, we end up in decline. Recline always leads to decline. Just think back to the first month of COVID. Too much telly. Too many crisps. Too much banana bread. . Recline turned into decline very quickly.

And it's not just during pandemics. People offend us, and our hearts recline. Family offends us, and our hearts recline. I was on holiday recently with eighteen of us in one Airbnb. Eighteen! Let me tell you, I had a couple of opportunities for my heart to recline that week. One bathroom. Eighteen people. That's not a holiday—that's sanctification.

If we don't deal with recline, our hearts get stuck in the wrong position. It's like what happened with my old car. Chantel reclined the passenger seat one day and it jammed. For a whole week it was stuck all the way back. Not a great look for a pastor rolling up to Maccas with his wife practically horizontal in the front seat. Or maybe people thought I was driving around town with a corpse. That's what happens spiritually when our hearts get stuck in recline—things start looking weird.

And here's the truth: When our heart is out of position, we make bad choices. Think back over your life. Your best decisions? They were made when your heart was inclined. Your worst decisions? Those were made when your heart was reclined. When our heart leans away from God, our choices lean away too.

That's why David says, "I have inclined my heart." He's saying, "I'm resetting my heart toward heaven." This isn't a one-time deal. It's not like a car alignment you do once and then forget about. This is daily maintenance.

When I was away those four weeks, I was asking God, "Show me where my heart's in recline." And can I be honest? It was hard. Just when I thought I was doing well, the Holy Spirit pointed out another area. Pride here. Cynicism there. A little offence hiding in the corner. It was humbling. But it was also freeing. Because every time He showed me an area, I had a chance to reset my heart back toward Him.

We don't just do this once. We don't just say, "Well, I inclined my heart back in 2003." No—this is daily. This is every morning, every decision, every conversation. A daily choice to recognise when our heart is drifting toward recline—and then to stand it back up toward God.

Because if we don't recognise it, we'll get stuck in it. But if we do recognise it, and we incline our hearts toward heaven, everything else in our life begins to align as well.

Will we recline back to our old position? Because here's the truth: Recline left unchecked always ends in decline. And life can decline quickly.

You ever reset your heart on a Sunday, only to find by Tuesday it's already reclined again? It happens. People come at Easter and Christmas for a quick reset, but it's not enough. We've got to daily set our hearts.

Check it. Incline it. Check it again. Incline it again.

Incline is a pre-decision. It's the choice we make before the choice. Before I go to bed—am I holding anything against anyone? Check it, incline it. Choosing joy instead of cynicism? Check it, incline it.

That's why this chapter is the foundation for the whole book. Because no matter what area we talk about, there will always be places in our hearts where we're tempted to recline.

Incline hurts. Just ask the treadmill. But the results are worth it. When we deal with our heart stuff, it stings—but the outcome is freedom. And the enemy hates nothing more than God's people walking free.

It's Okay to Hate Decline

Psalm 119:113 (NKJV) says, "I hate the double-minded, but I love Your law."

Now that's strong. David uses a word we don't usually associate with church life: *hate.* It's not exactly the kind of word we put on a fridge magnet or a bumper sticker. And I'll be honest with you—in twenty-five years of preaching, I don't think I've ever used *hate* in a positive way. Certainly not as a main point. Hate is a strong word.

But here's what's fascinating: David uses hate before he uses love. He says, "I hate the double-minded, but I love Your law." He's being brutally honest about the struggle inside him. He's saying, "I hate what a divided, half-hearted posture produces in me. I hate that I'm constantly pulled between incline and recline. I hate the tug-of-war in my soul."

Can anyone else relate? Because I can. I know where my heart should be. I know what I should do, what I should say. And yet, I still mess it up. I know I shouldn't hang on to what they said, what they did, what I did—but I can't let go.

Often before we can change, we have to hate what a reclined heart is doing to us. Did you know sometimes it's actually hate that pushes us to change more than love does?

Think about working out. I don't always love going to the gym. What I do love is the feeling after. But what really gets me there? I hate the feeling of not working out more than I love the thought of working out. That hatred of how I feel when I skip it—that's what drives me to lace up my trainers.

Same with forgiveness. Do I always love the idea of forgiving someone? No! But I hate the way bitterness feels in my heart even more. That's what drives me to forgive.

I hate the way I keep going back to old habits. I hate the way anger poisons my marriage. I hate the aftertaste of self-pity. I hate what double-mindedness does to me, to my relationships, to my life.

Hatred can become holy fuel for change.

Here's the challenge though: Most of the time we actually love the way recline feels. Let's be real. I love a recliner! Put me in a La-Z-Boy chair, Diet Coke on the side, remote in one hand, peanut M&Ms on my lap—that's heaven. Recline feels amazing for a moment. But if that's where we live? That's dangerous.

Because life hurts. People offend us. Things don't go our way. And when our heart slips into recline as the default setting, it gets risky. Because recline leads to decline. And decline eventually destroys us.

When David says, "I hate the double-minded," he's not saying he hates people. He's not saying he hates himself. He's saying, "I hate this posture in me. I hate where it takes me. I hate what it does to my heart."

And maybe that's where some of us need to get to. A place where we're willing to admit, "I hate what this bitterness is doing to me. I hate the anger that keeps wrecking my relationships. I hate the self-pity that steals my joy. I hate the compromise that keeps pulling me back."

Because until we hate what a reclined heart produces, we'll keep living there. But when we start to hate it—really hate it—we'll finally find the grit to change.

> Until we hate what a reclined heart produces, we'll keep living there.

Can I be honest for a sec, like David? We've actually got to start hating recline.

Not the feeling—the outcome.

Because let's be real: A reclined heart often feels brilliant in the moment. It's comfortable. It's easy. It's like sinking into a sofa with a takeaway and pretending calories don't exist. But the outcome? That's where the pain shows up.

And if we go one step further—we've got to start hating sin. Psalm 97:10 says, "Let those who love the Lord hate evil." Strong language. But necessary. Because until we hate the effect of sin, we'll keep flirting with it.

You've got to hate being drunk in order to stop. Not the buzz, not the laugh with your mates, but the next day—the regret, the headache, the "never again" that you say every Saturday morning.

You've got to hate looking at those websites late at night. Not the rush in the moment, but the shame after. The way it makes you feel like you're hiding from God and everyone else.

You've got to hate insecurity enough to finally change. I'll be honest—that's been my battle. For years, I lived off the validation of social media. But I reached a point where I hated what it was doing *in* me more than I loved what it did *for* me. That hatred drove me to change.

See the pattern? It's not the feelings—it's the outcomes.

The apostle Paul basically summed it up in Romans 7:15: "I do not understand what I do. For what I want to do I do not do, but what I hate I do." That's me some days. That's probably you too.

At some point, we've got to hate recline more than we love incline. Because here's the truth: Until we hate something more than we love something, we won't change.

The Israelites had to hate Egypt more than they loved Egypt in order to step into the Promised Land. And that's tough, because Egypt had its perks—familiarity, predictability, a few creature comforts. The devil will whisper, "One more night in Egypt won't hurt. One more day with the old crew. One more step back into the past." But one more night in Egypt is always one night too many.

We've got to hate our past more than we love it. Hate the compromise. Hate the bitterness. Hate the shame. Hate the duplicity. Not in a self-loathing way, but in a holy way that says: I'm done letting this define me.

David said, "I hate the double-minded." And that's exactly how it feels. We love what it does for us in the moment, but we hate what it does to us afterwards.

Until we hate sin more than we love the feeling it gives us, we'll never make the change. But once we do—once hate becomes holy fuel—we find the courage to finally step out of recline and start inclining our hearts toward God.

Embracing the Incline

Psalm 119:113 (NKJV) says, "I hate the double-minded, but I love Your law."

David doesn't just stop at what he hates. He goes on to say what he loves—God's Word. He gives us the key to an inclined heart: the Holy Scriptures.

Who here loves that feeling after you've done the right thing? After you've dragged yourself to the gym, or finally gone for that walk, or chosen the salad instead of the chips. The hard part is the decision, but the payoff always feels worth it. That's exactly what David is talking about. An inclined heart is built by daily choosing God's Word.

Incline means "upward." It moves our life higher. When our hearts are in recline, the only thing that can change our posture back to incline is the Word of God. Nothing else has that power.

Who loves the feeling after spending time in His Word? It's like spiritual oxygen. But let's be honest—the Bible is a battlefield. It's like the treadmill—it's a daily uphill choice. It takes discipline. Every day we fight the distractions, the to-do lists, the noise, the endless scrolling. Everything in life pulls us away from incline.

That's why falling in love with God's Word matters so much. And here's the thing—we can read it enough to ease our conscience, but not enough to fall in love with it. That's the danger. When the Bible becomes a tickbox, it won't incline our heart. But when we actually love it, it starts to overflow in everyday life.

I know I'm in love with the Word when it begins to come out of my mouth naturally, without me even trying. When a TV presenter signs off saying, "Do not let your hearts be troubled," my first thought is, *That's John 14:1!* When I see someone sick, the first verse that comes to mind is, "By His stripes we are healed" (Isaiah 53:5 NKJV). When I meet someone in lack, I speak Philippians 4:19: "My God shall supply all your need according to His riches in glory" (NKJV).

Even in the everyday stuff—when I feel anger rising, I hear, "Be angry and sin not." When I'm tempted to go to bed still annoyed, the Word whispers, "Do not let the sun go down on your wrath" (Ephesians 4:26 NKJV). When I feel the pull toward sin, it's Psalm 119:11 (NKJV) that surfaces: "Your word I have hidden in my heart, that I might not sin against You."

Whatever we store up in our hearts will eventually spill out into our lives. Junk in, junk out. Word in, Word out.

Here's the Challenge:

Let's stop nibbling at Scripture just enough to keep guilt away. Let's fall in love with it all over again. Let's make God's Word the daily incline that re-postures our heart.

Because when we store up this treasure, it won't just stay hidden—it will flow out into every conversation, every decision, and every corner of our lives.

Question:
Holy Spirit, What Are You Saying to Me?

The reclined heart can only be healed through two things: union with God and honest conversations with others.

First, **union**. When we open His Word, we open our hearts to His presence. On holiday, God spoke something simple but sharp to me: "Jon, don't be more familiar with a secular song than the Word of God." That hit me. Because I don't want to be the guy who can belt out every Oasis or Coldplay anthem word for word, but can't recall a single verse of Scripture.

> Whatever we store up in our hearts will eventually spill out into our lives.

Jesus said in Luke 6:45, "The mouth speaks what the heart is full of." In other words, what comes out of me is proof of what's inside me. If my mouth is full of dirty humour, it's because my heart is unclean. If my mouth is full of God's promises, it's because my heart is full of faith.

How do we fight the enemy of recline? Through daily union with God. By confessing His Word, speaking His promises, reminding our soul of His truth. Because the truth will always outlive a lie. He is the Vine and we are the branches. And we only stay alive, only stay fruitful, when we remain connected to Him.

Second, **honest conversations**. Because when God starts working on our heart, His Word often brings hidden things to the surface. And sometimes what comes up surprises us. The problem is, we don't always have the tools to deal with it on our own.

That reminds me of a fishing trip I took with my son Justice while we were on holiday. We went down to the pier with nothing but a hired rod and a bit of bait. As he cast out, I found myself praying, "Lord, please don't let him catch anything." Not because I didn't want him to have fun, but because I had no idea what we'd do if something actually took the bait! We didn't have a landing net, a keep net—none of the proper tools. I was quietly panicking that a fish might come up we weren't ready for.

And that's exactly what can happen in our spiritual life. When God's Word goes to work, things rise to the surface—hurts, habits, offences. But unless we're equipped with the right tools, we won't know how to handle them. That's why the rest of this book is about just that: giving us the practical tools to deal with what surfaces, so that when God reveals something in our heart, we don't just throw it back—we let Him clean it, heal it, and use it.

A Prayer for an Inclined Heart

Holy Spirit,

Thank You for showing me the true posture of my heart.
Where I have grown comfortable in recline,
give me the courage to incline my heart back toward You.

Help me recognise when my heart drifts,
and give me the strength to redirect it daily.
Teach me to hate what pulls me away from You
and to love what draws me closer to Your truth.

Search my heart.
Heal what is wounded.
Expose what needs changing.
And give me an understanding heart, like Solomon asked for.

Today, I choose incline.
I choose Your Word.
I choose freedom.

In Jesus's name, amen.

CHAPTER 2

The Hard Heart

Matthew 13 marks a clear shift in Jesus's ministry. Up until this point, He's been teaching in synagogues, reasoning with people, and laying out the truth of the kingdom in fairly straightforward terms. But as opposition begins to rise—particularly from the religious leaders—Jesus starts teaching in parables.

The disciples are curious. "Why the change, Jesus? Why tell stories instead of giving us the straight teaching?"

Jesus replies, "You are permitted to understand the secrets of the Kingdom of Heaven, but others are not. To those who listen to my teaching, more understanding will be given. But to those who are not listening, even what little understanding they have will be taken away" (Matthew 13:11–12 NLT).

In other words, some people are wide open and hungry to hear from God. Others . . . not so much. They've hardened their hearts. And here's the thing about a hard heart: It's not an ear problem. It's not even an intelligence problem. It's a heart problem.

As we read this our first response is probably, "That's not me . . . *right?*"

Now, whenever we hear a sermon or read a book about hard hearts, we immediately start building a mental guest list of everyone else who really needs to hear this.

- Your boss, definitely.

- Your spouse? You're nudging them with your elbow right now, hoping they're paying attention.

- Your teenage son or daughter? Let's not even go there.

I'll be honest—when I started putting this series together, that was my reaction too. But then God did what God often does—He turned the spotlight back on me. Here's what I've come to realise: At the end of the day . . .

1. My heart is my responsibility.

2. I can't control other people.
    *   People will say things.
    *   They'll write things.
    *   Some will even intentionally try to hurt me, but whether those things harden my heart—that's my choice.

You see, a hard heart doesn't usually happen overnight. It's not like one bad day and suddenly you've turned into a hard-hearted Harry (sorry if your name is Harry). It happens slowly. A disappointment here. A betrayal there. A prayer that didn't get answered the way you hoped. A person who let you down. Each little knock adds another layer around the heart. It's been said that bitterness is a life sentence without parole.

Before long, we're not as tender toward God as we used to be. We're not as quick to forgive. We don't feel as deeply. We're cautious, closed off, maybe even cynical. That's what Jesus was getting at when He quoted Isaiah:

> "For the hearts of these people are hardened, and their ears cannot hear, and they have closed their eyes." (Matthew 13:15 NLT)

It's not that God stopped speaking. It's that people stopped listening. When I played football, our physio would always say, "Your body tells the truth." If you're limping, you can't just say, "Nah, I'm fine." Your body never lies!

The same is true spiritually. Your heart tells the truth. If you find yourself easily offended, quick to criticise, slow to forgive—that's not just a personality quirk. That's a heart issue.

And just like I had to take responsibility for my fitness back on the pitch, I have to take responsibility for my heart now.

God's Heart for Your Heart

The good news is this: God doesn't want us living with a hardened heart. That's not His plan. He wants to soften it, heal it, and make it whole again.

Ezekiel prophesied that God would one day take away hearts of stone and replace them with hearts of flesh (Ezekiel 36:26). Jesus is the fulfilment of that promise. He's still in the business of softening hearts today.

So if you recognise any hardness creeping in, don't despair. Don't shrug it off either. Bring it to Him. Ask Him to make you tender again—to open your eyes, unstop your ears, and give you a heart that beats in rhythm with His.

So how do you know if your heart is hardening? Jesus actually gives us five signs in Matthew 13. Think of it as a spiritual checkup.

Five Symptoms of a Hard Heart

Inability to Receive

Jesus said, "To those who listen to my teaching, more understanding will be given" (v. 12 NLT).

The first sign of a hard heart is that we stop receiving from others. We become wise in our own opinions. We put our guard up. Instead of being teachable, we're untouchable.

If anyone says something that doesn't fit with how we think it should be, we dismiss it. "Nope. That's not right. Doesn't line up with my opinion, so I'm not listening."

My dad used to tell me all the time: "You can learn from a fool, Jon, but a fool can't learn from anyone." That's always stuck with me. A humble heart can learn from anyone. A proud heart refuses to learn from anyone.

Think about it: The disciples didn't always get it right. They asked daft questions. They misunderstood Jesus. But at least they were open enough to receive. That's why they grew. Meanwhile, the Pharisees had memorised entire chunks of Scripture but couldn't receive what was right in front of them.

Here's the question: Are we still open to receive? Can we still learn from people—even those we don't agree with?

> A humble heart can learn from anyone. A proud heart refuses to learn from anyone.

Inability to Hear

Jesus goes on: "Their ears cannot hear" (v. 15 NLT).

A hardened heart doesn't just stop receiving from people—it also stops hearing from God.

God speaks through His Word. He speaks through His Spirit. And He speaks through His people. Sometimes the most inconvenient people! But if my heart is hard, I'll miss it every time.

Let me be honest with you. In eleven years of leading a church, my heart has only hardened for an extended period of time twice. Once was during COVID. The other time . . . well maybe that's for another day.

COVID—I don't even like saying or reading the word now. It's hard to even imagine what we all went through. Overnight we had to close the doors of our churches. People were divided. Should we gather? Should we wear masks? Should we sing? Should we take vaccine? Should we hit the NHS pots and pans on a Thursday night for those living in the UK? Everyone had an opinion. And all those opinions were different.

Our board chairman, Richard, said something in the middle of all the chaos: "This will be the making of us as a church; it's the greatest opportunity ever to love our community." At the time, I brushed it off. I was tired, frustrated, and—if I'm honest—a bit cynical. But fast-forward a year later, I realised something: That wasn't just Richard speaking. That was the Holy Spirit speaking through him. But because my heart was hard, I couldn't hear it. All I could hear was the noise and chaos in my own head. That's the danger. When our heart hardens, God might be speaking clearly—but all we hear is our own feelings. As I reflect back on that time, Richard was right. It really was the beginning of God using our church to be a blessing to our city and beyond. As a result of pandemic and the tireless work of our staff and volunteers we were able to hand out over 3 million meals to our local community.

Inability to See

Jesus goes on to say: "They have closed their eyes—so their eyes cannot see" (v. 15 NLT).

When the heart hardens, vision fades. You can't see clearly anymore. Life becomes all about me: my problems, my struggles, my disappointments.

When we first moved to Cape Town in 2014 to be part of the Hillsong Church plant there, I'll never forget the shock of driving from the airport and seeing people begging on the side of the road and at the traffic light. The well-meaning gentleman who picked us up that sunny afternoon said to just ignore them: "You'll get used to it." I was shocked, Chantel and I made a decision we weren't going to get used to it. We would play our part in trying to make a small difference where we could. It broke something open inside of us. But when our heart gets hard, we stop seeing the people who need us most. Our vision shrinks down so it's simply just all about us: our needs, our issues, our opinions. We lose sight!

And if I'm honest, that's usually my first warning sign. When my world gets small—when I'm only focused on myself—it's a red flag that my heart is hardening.

Inability to Understand

Jesus adds: "Their hearts cannot understand" (v. 15 NLT).

A hard heart doesn't try to understand. It judges quickly. It assumes the worst. But here's the truth: People often treat us the way they've been treated. If they were treated unfairly with disrespect growing up, often this repeats itself in later life. This doesn't make it right, but it makes sense.

If we knew the pain of someone's past, we'd have far more sympathy for their present.

I wonder how many times we've judged someone without knowing their hidden battles. Maybe they were rude to us, but we didn't know they'd been up all night with a sick child. Maybe they seemed cold, but I had no idea they were carrying grief.

Stephen Covey famously wrote: "Seek first to understand, then to be understood."[1] That's wisdom. A soft heart seeks to understand

Inability to Change

Finally, Jesus says: "They cannot turn to me and let me heal them" (v. 15 NLT).

The last and most dangerous symptom of a hard heart is the refusal to change. Jesus recognises in this verse that so often we get stuck. We dig in our heels. We say, "This is just who I am. I'm not changing."

One of my biggest fears as a leader is that I get stuck. I cling to old ways, old methods, old mindsets, old leadership practices. Thank God for young people in my world—they keep me on my toes! They challenge me to think differently, to adapt, to stay fresh. My daughter will often say to me, "Dad, are you *really* leaving the house in that outfit?" Often she has a point!

God is always doing a new thing. Isaiah 43:19 says: "See, I am doing a new thing! Now it springs up; do you not perceive it?" The danger is that we don't perceive it—because our hearts are too hard. We're so attached to what *was* that we miss what *is*.

If we knew the pain of someone's past, we'd have far more sympathy for their present.

---

[1] Stephen R. Covey, *The 7 Habits of Highly Effective People: Restoring the Character Ethic* (Free Press, 2004), 235.

But here's the good news: Nobody is too old to change. Nobody is too far gone. Whatever our age, our habits, our history—Jesus can still make all things new. The only question is: Will we let Him?

Quick recap—the five symptoms of a hard heart:

1. Inability to receive

2. Inability to hear

3. Inability to see

4. Inability to understand

5. Inability to change

Now, who would be honest enough to say, "I can see myself in at least one of those?" I certainly can. Maybe we've stopped receiving. Maybe we've stopped hearing. Maybe our vision's gone cloudy. Maybe we've lost empathy. Or maybe we've dug in our heels and said, "I'm not changing."

The point isn't to feel condemned. Jesus isn't trying to embarrass us. He's inviting us to turn to Him and be healed. Because the same Jesus who exposes the problem also gives us the solution. "They cannot turn to me and let me heal them." That's the key. If you turn to Him, He will heal you.

Let Him Heal You

What if the greatest barrier to the power of God in our lives—and in our churches—isn't the culture, the government, or even the devil? What if it's our own hardened hearts? That thought scares me. But it also gives me hope. Because if my heart is the problem, then my heart can change. And God specialises in heart change.

Ezekiel 36:26 (NLT) is one of my favourite promises: "I will give you a new heart, and I will put a new spirit in you. I will take out your stony, stubborn heart and give you a tender, responsive heart."

That's what He wants to do for you and for me. So here's the invitation: Don't just nod along as you read this book. Don't just agree in theory.

Turn to Him as you turn the pages and let Him soften your heart. Let Him heal you.

Maybe you've been carrying offence for too long. Maybe disappointment has calloused you. Maybe cynicism has crept in. Whatever it is, Jesus is able to make your heart new again.

How to Heal a Hardened Heart

The Bible doesn't just show us the symptoms of a hardened heart; it shows us how to heal a hardened heart.

We've seen in Matthew 13 how Jesus diagnosed the problem: hard hearts. The religious leaders had resisted Him, the crowds weren't really hearing, and even His closest disciples struggled to understand. But before Jesus ever explained the symptoms, He actually told a story about the cure.

"A farmer went out to sow his seed." (13:3)

You probably know the story. Some seed fell on the path, some on rocky ground, some among thorns, and some on good soil. The first three failed. The last one flourished.

Here's the key: The seed was the same. The difference was the soil.

Jesus explains later that the seed is the Word of God. That means the issue isn't the power of God's Word—it works. The issue is the condition of the heart it lands in.

If you are anything like me, from time to time our hearts can harden, so how can we heal a hardened heart? Jesus gives us three clear steps.

Examine the Grounds of Our Hearts

The first step is humility. We've have to stop pointing fingers and start looking inward.

Psalm 139:23 (NLT) says, "Search me, O God, and know my heart; test me and know my anxious thoughts."

The farmer scatters the same seed everywhere, but it lands on four types of ground:

1. *The Path* – The birds swoop down and steal the seed before it even sinks in. Jesus says that's the enemy distracting us. For some of us, it's already happening. The Word is being preached, but our phones distract us, our mind wanders, and before we know it, the Word has been stolen.

   We've have to stop pointing fingers and start looking inward.

2. *The Rocky Places* – The seed springs up quickly but withers because it has no root. That's the shallow heart—excited at first but easily offended. As soon as pressure comes, it falls away.

3. *The Thorny Ground* – The seed grows, but the thorns choke it. Jesus says that's sin and the worries of life. Pride, greed, lust, envy—secret sins we think we can manage but which always end up managing us. As I often say, don't play with sin; you never win.

4. *The Good Soil* – This is the heart that receives the Word honestly, humbly, and consistently. And the result is fruit: thirty, sixty, even a hundredfold harvest.

Notice the pattern? The enemy hardens our hearts in three main ways: *Distraction*, *Offence*, and *Sin*. I call it DOS (not the old Microsoft operating system).

Life will always hand us opportunities for DOS. Someone says something hurtful—will I take offence? The world shouts for my attention—will I let distraction steal my focus? Temptation knocks—will I give in?

The ground of my heart is my responsibility. If I want to see fruit, I've got to examine the soil.

Expose the Weeds and Rocks

Once we've examined our hearts, the next step is to expose what doesn't belong there. You can't plant a new bush without first pulling out the weeds—my good friend and garden enthusiast Graeme Hollinger taught me this. Which brings us back to DOS.

- *Distraction* – What's stealing your attention from reading God's Word? Maybe it's endless scrolling on your phone. I know for me this can be a real challenge. Maybe it's overworking. Maybe it's just busyness. Distraction is one of the enemy's favourite tools, because if he can't destroy you, he'll simply distract you.

- *Offence* – Who are you holding a grudge against? Offence is like carrying a backpack full of cement. It weighs you down, slows you down, and eventually breaks you down. Jesus said, "Blessed are the peacemakers." That means I can't afford to carry offence; however hard it is, the goal is to ask God help me make peace and forgive. Physical healing heals the body, but forgiveness heals the SOUL.

> Distraction is one of the enemy's favourite tools, because if he can't destroy you, he'll simply distract you.

- *Sin* – Where have you let compromise creep in? Pride? Greed? Lust? Envy? Romans 6:14 declares, "For sin shall not have dominion over you" (NKJV). That's a promise, but it's also a challenge. Don't flirt with sin. Don't justify it. Expose it and bring it into the light.

Here's the truth: God's grace covers us, but His Word still calls us to holiness. The good news is that we don't have to fight this battle alone. The Holy Spirit helps us. He convicts us gently—not to shame us but to free us.

Exchange Stubborn Soil for Good Soil

Finally, we make an exchange. We bring God our stubborn, calloused, rocky soil, and He gives us a soft, responsive heart.

Ezekiel 36:26 says, "I will give you a new heart and put a new spirit in you; I will remove from you your heart of stone and give you a heart of flesh."

That's the cure. You can't fix your own heart by sheer willpower. You've got to let God do the surgery. Good soil is simply a humble, honest, responsive heart. It's a heart that says:

- "God, I'm open."

- "God, I'm listening."

- "God, I'm willing to change."

And when that happens, the harvest comes. Because remember: The seed is never the problem. The Word of God always works. The question is: Will my heart will let it in?

When I was playing footballer, and not a very good one, the physio used to tell me: "Your body never lies." You can pretend you're fine, but if you're limping, everyone knows you're not.

The same is true spiritually. Your heart never lies. You might say you're fine, but the fruit in your life tells the real story. If you're bitter, easily offended, always distracted, or stuck in sin, it's a heart issue.

But just like an athlete doesn't stay injured forever—there's recovery, rehab, and renewal—our hearts can heal too.

Some of us want the blessing, the fruit, the favour of God on our lives. We want the exciting bits—the hundredfold harvest. But the fruit isn't determined by the seed. The Word of God is unchanging, powerful, effective. The fruit is determined by the soil.

And the soil is *our* responsibility.

If your life isn't producing the fruit you long for, don't blame the seed. Don't blame the sower. Ask God to examine the soil.

Time to Break Up the Hardened Ground

So, what do we do when we've examined the soil of our hearts and realised—if we're honest—it's a little crusty? Maybe even solid like concrete?

Here's the truth: Every single one of us gets to a crossroads. We face disappointment, betrayal, distraction, or sin, and then we have a choice. Do we get bitter, or do we get better? That's the daily choice.

I wish I could tell you that the ground softens itself over time. But it doesn't. Unless we take responsibility for our hearts, they don't just stay the same—they harden.

I know, because I've been there.

If we allow distraction, offence, and sin (remember the "DOS" from earlier?) to linger too long, they calcify. They set like concrete. And eventually, they stop the Word of God from penetrating at all.

So how do we break up hard ground?

The Bible says in John 7:38 (NLT): "Rivers of living water will flow from his heart."

That's the secret. The only thing that breaks hard ground is water. Living water. The presence of God poured over our lives.

> Unless we take responsibility for our hearts, they don't just stay the same— they harden.

Let me show you five ways we can pour that living water over our hearts.

1. Water with Worship

Worship is one of the most powerful heart-softeners I know. Because here's what happens when I worship:

- I switch the face of the person who has hurt me with the face of my Saviour.

- I exchange my issue for His love.

- I trade my mess for His grace.

- I surrender my past for His promise.

I can't stay in God's presence for very long with a hard heart. Neither can you. When I worship, I make a holy exchange: what others have done to me for what Jesus did for me. And that changes everything. You see, worship lifts my eyes from what's been done against me and fixes them on what's been done for me. And suddenly, the offence or pain that felt so heavy loses its power.

That's why worship is the best antidote to a hard heart. I can't tell you how many times, I've been holding on to something then I say to Alexa, "Play worship music," and as I allow the words to wash over my heart, it begins to soften and I start regaining perspective.

And here's the key: Worship doesn't start when the band starts playing on a Sunday. Worship is a daily posture. It's me saying, "God, I'm giving You the first look. I'm putting You above my pain, my worry, my agenda, here's my heart."

Sometimes, the very moment I don't feel like worshipping is the exact moment I need to worship the most. That's when the ground really starts to break open.

2. Water with Forgiveness

Five chapters later on in Matthew 18, Peter comes to Jesus with the question we all secretly want to ask: "How often should I forgive someone who sins against me? Seven times?" (v. 21 NLT).

Peter thought he was being generous. Seven strikes and you're out—that's more than fair, right? But Jesus replies: "No, not seven times, but seventy times seven!" (v. 22 NLT).

In other words, stop counting. Forgiveness isn't about keeping score. It's about losing count.

Imagine forgiving someone 490 times in one day—that's once every two minutes! Jesus wasn't giving us a mathematics lesson. He was giving us a heart lesson. He was saying: "Don't stop forgiving, because unforgiveness is one of the quickest ways to harden your heart."

Let me share with you a personal story from my wife's family. In 2018 Chantel's dad was tragically murdered in a drive-by shooting in East Los Angeles. Chantel had only a few years earlier reconnected with him.

> Forgiveness isn't about keeping score. It's about losing count.

The pain she suffered for many months was unbearable to watch. At the wake Chantel connected with some extended relatives. One of her distant cousins pulled Chantel aside and said, "We're just waiting for the right moment to get revenge—we know who is responsible, we will make it right for your dad."

That broke Chantel. This man had been carrying hurt, and instead of releasing it, he was rehearsing it. He wasn't living; he was waiting to take revenge. Chantel ministered to him that day about forgiveness. She said, "You can't keep score. You've got to let go. If you take revenge, then the cycle of hatred and killing continues. You see, forgiveness is not weakness—it's freedom." Supernaturally the family member received her love which ultimately came from the Father.

I can tell you firsthand: The fruit that's growing out of Chantel's life today is directly connected to her forgiving heart. Unforgiveness doesn't just keep us in chains; it stops new life from growing. But when we forgive, we water our hearts and prepare the soil for God's seed to flourish.

3. Water with Honesty

Sometimes, the first step toward softening our hearts is simply admitting where we're at.

Truthfully, the British stiff upper lip isn't always the most spiritual gift. I can say that because I am a Brit. Some of us have perfected the art of saying, "I'm fine," when we're anything but fine.

But here's the truth: Hard ground softens when we get honest.

First, be honest with God. "Search me, O God, and know my heart" (Psalm 139:23 NLT). There's alot to admire about David's leadership and his heart after God, but for me it's his unwavering honesty. He asks God to search his heart for anything which could be lurking to harm him.

Then, be honest with others. That might mean talking to a trusted friend, a mentor, or a local church pastor, someone you can be completely open and transparent with.

Worship opens our hearts to be vulnerable, but honesty keeps them soft. Sometimes the bravest thing you can do is say, "I'm struggling. Can we chat? Will you pray with me?"

Honesty cracks the ground wide open so the water can seep in.

4. Water with Gratitude

Psalm 111:1 (NKJV) says: "I will praise the LORD with my whole heart."

Gratitude is another key that pours water onto hard ground.

Something shifts in my heart when I start thanking God. Even for the small things, especially for the small things. Gratitude for small things is like rain for the soil of the heart. When was the last time you thanked God for breath in your lungs? For the friend who checked in on you? For the cup of Yorkshire tea that tasted exactly right?

5. Water with Hope

Finally, hope keeps our hearts soft. Last year, I sat down with a dear friend, Coach Mullins from Florida. He's an eighty-one-young American football coach and he is as tough as nails, yet he has the softest heart. We talked about church, family, football, politics—you name it, we covered it all. And do you know what he told me in our time together?

"Jon, the secret to longevity in this life is keep looking for the good— even in the bad."

That stuck with me. Hope is about scanning the horizon for God's goodness, even when life looks bleak. It's believing Romans 8:28: "In all things God works for the good of those who love him."

Hope is a choice. A daily decision to say, "I believe there's good in this situation, because I believe God is still working."

And when I look for the good, I find it. It might be small, but it's always there.

Here's the Challenge:

So how do we break up hard ground? With worship, forgiveness, honesty, gratitude, and hope.

Each one pours living water over our hearts. Each one prepares the soil so that the Word of God can go in deep and produce a harvest. Because here's the thing: The seed is always powerful. The Word of God never fails. The question isn't the seed—it's the soil. And soft ground always produces fruit.

God is in the business of transforming hearts—from hardness to wholeness, from barrenness to blessing. And He will do it, if you let Him.

Question:
Holy Spirit, What Are You Saying to Me?

Maybe your heart is in a good place and already soft. Praise God! But maybe parts of it are still hard. The good news is that it's never too late. God can soften stone. He can bring life where there's been dryness. He can cause fruit to grow where once there was barrenness.

You don't have to figure this out in a single moment. Start small. Examine, soften, sow. Take one area of your life today and allow God's living water to flow in.

And as you do, remember: Soft hearts bear good fruit. Hard hearts bear bad fruit. God is in the business of transforming hearts—from hardness to wholeness, from barrenness to blessing. And He will do it, if you let Him.

A Prayer for a New Heart

Heavenly Father,

Thank You for loving me even when my heart has grown hard.
Thank You that Your Word still carries power and purpose.

Today I ask You to give me a new heart—soft, open, and responsive to You again.
Remove the parts that have become cold or closed off.
Heal the places that have been hurt or disappointed.
Forgive me where distraction, offence, or sin have hardened me.

Holy Spirit, pour Your living water over my soul.
Soften the soil of my heart so Your truth can take root and grow.
Where I've built walls, help me tear them down.
Where I've held on to bitterness, teach me to forgive.

Lord, let my life bear good fruit—love, peace, joy, and kindness.
Help me to stay thankful, humble, and teachable.
I trust that Your Word will accomplish its purpose in me,
and that new life will grow from even the hardest places.

In the precious name of Jesus, amen.

CHAPTER 3

The Pure in Heart

In this chapter I want to unpack a chamber of the heart that seems to be talked about less and less in culture and especially in churches amongst believers today—purity. Don't all skip to the next chapter ;-)

The word *purity* comes from the Greek word *katharos*, from which we get the word *catharsis*. It means a cleansing—not just of the body, but of the heart, mind, and emotions. God's heart is that our hearts would be continually cleansed and made pure. He's not after a one-time cleanup; He's after a lifelong process of renewal.

When you look around our world today, it's easy to see the moral slide. You can almost feel it. The lines that once seemed clear have become blurred. As society moves further and further away from the Bible, we see that what was once celebrated as pure is now mocked, and what was once considered distorted is normalised. The prophet Isaiah saw this coming nearly 2,500 years ago:

> Woe to those who call evil good
>   and good evil,
> who put darkness for light
>   and light for darkness. (Isaiah 5:20 NKJV)

But this shouldn't surprise us—it's the enemy's oldest trick. **The devil's ways have always been to take what is pure and distort it. God's way has always been to take what is distorted and make it pure.**

That's the great reversal of the gospel. God doesn't run from impurity; He redeems it.

He takes what's broken, twisted, and ashamed, and washes it clean. He restores purity where the world only sees ruin.

God doesn't run from impurity; He redeems it.

Whenever we live contrary to God's Word, impurities begin to build up in our lives. Like a river blocked by debris, our hearts can become cluttered—not just with sin, but with distraction, pride, fear, comparison, or resentment. The problem isn't that we've stopped loving God; it's that our love has become divided.

Sadly, the heart isn't one-dimensional. You can be free in one area but still messed up in another. You might have forgiven someone who hurt you but still wrestle with impurity in your thoughts. You might be serving God faithfully yet quietly carrying bitterness or insecurity. That's why David prayed, "Search me, O God, and know my heart. . . . Point out anything in me that offends you, and lead me along the path of everlasting life" (Psalm 139:23–24 NLT).

Spiritual maturity isn't about having a perfect heart; it's about having a surrendered one. It's allowing God to examine every corner, not just the ones we're comfortable showing. True purity isn't achieved through hiding but being honest before God. Sometimes because of the nature and shame of our thoughts we feel like we could never be honest with our spouse, family, or even closest friends, but Jesus can handle every one of our deepest, darkest, and dirtiest thoughts. As you are reading this chapter, surrender them over to Jesus, allow His light to come in and shine, not house dark places. Jesus will also never hold any of our thoughts against us. He wants to take them off us so we can be free.

You see, purity isn't just about what you say no to; it's about what you say yes to. It's not a restrictive word; it's a freeing one. A pure heart is one that is fully alive to God, undistracted by guilt, shame, or duplicity. It's the kind of heart that can see clearly, love deeply, and hear God's voice without distortion.

The pure in heart are those who say, "Lord, don't just forgive me, transform me. Don't just wash my hands, cleanse my motives. Don't just change what I do, change why I do it."

Purity sharpens your vision and softens your spirit.

Our world may be obsessed with appearance, but God still looks at the heart. And when He finds one that's pure—not perfect, but honest and surrendered—that's where His presence loves to dwell.

In Matthew 5, we find a sequence of nine blessings Jesus spoke in what's known as the Sermon on the Mount—the Beatitudes. Each one describes the kind of heart and attitude that leads to divine favour and true happiness in God's kingdom. Jesus wasn't just giving motivational sayings here; He was painting a picture of the kind of people who carry heaven's values on earth.

"Blessed are the pure in heart, for they will see God." (Matthew 5:8)

If Jesus had simply said, "Blessed are the pure, for they will see God," the religious people of His day would've been delighted. They were experts at outward purity. They had a rule for everything—what to eat, what to wear, how far you could walk on the Sabbath. They spent all their energy making the outside look spotless, but Jesus saw right through it. They were washing the cup on the outside while the inside was filthy—when I say filthy I mean *filthy*.

God is far more concerned about the purity of our hearts than the platform of our lives.

Jesus wasn't impressed by appearance. He went deeper, straight to the heart. Because real purity doesn't start with our behaviour; it starts with our motives.

You can't clean your heart by polishing your habits.

The world says, "Fix yourself up, try harder, perform better." But Jesus says, "Let Me make you new from the inside out."

That's why He said, "Blessed are the pure in heart." Not the gifted in heart, not the powerful in heart, not the influential in heart, not the qualified in heart—but the pure in heart.

God is far more concerned about the purity of our hearts than the platform of our lives.

We often get it the other way around. We celebrate gifting, charisma, and talent. We love power—the power of people's words, their influence, their social media following.

The church, at times, has mistaken power for purity. But Jesus never said, "Blessed are the powerful." He said, "Blessed are the pure in heart."

Purity means having an undivided heart—one that isn't trying to please God and the crowd at the same time. It's a heart that says, "God, I want what You want." It's not perfection; it's authenticity. When we're pure in heart, we're quick to repent, quick to say sorry, quick to forgive. We keep short accounts.

As we move closer to the return of Christ, I believe purity will once again take centre stage. Not the showy kind that tries to impress, but the quiet kind that lives to please and glorify God. It will be the pure who see God—not just in eternity but here on earth right now.

When your heart is pure, you see God's hand at work in your everyday life. You recognise His presence in people, His goodness in creation, His guidance in the small moments. Purity clears the lens through which we see God.

Purity matters to God, and it's where true blessing begins.

And here's the promise in the verse: They will see God. When your heart is pure, you begin to see Him everywhere—in the ordinary, in nature, in the people you meet, in the quiet moments where He whispers peace.

What Exactly Is Purity?

Purity is the nature and character of Jesus being formed in me.

It's not a personality type or a moral checklist. It's Christ being fully alive in my inner world—His nature shaping my nature, His desires shaping my desires, His motives becoming mine.

John Piper once said, "Jesus did not come into the world simply because we had some bad habits that need to be broken. He came into the world because we have such dirty hearts that need to be purified."[2]

That gets right to the point. Jesus didn't come to polish up our behaviour; He came to transform our hearts. He's not interested in cosmetic Christianity—that's called Religion. He's after genuine change, the kind that starts deep within and works its way out.

Purity isn't just about avoiding wrong things; it's about being filled with the right things. It's not just saying no to sin; it's saying yes to Jesus in every area of life. When His Spirit fills your heart, He doesn't just cleanse what's unclean; He replaces it with what's holy, true, and beautiful.

The pure heart is one that says, "God, I want to want what You want." It's not about perfection, it's about direction.

Purity isn't passive; it's intentional.

Every day, the Holy Spirit wants to direct our thoughts, our motives, our decisions, but we have to give Him permission. That can be simply saying one of the oldest prayers in our Christian faith—"Come, Holy Spirit." That simple invitation creates a pathway to purity in our everyday.

> Purity isn't just about avoiding wrong things; it's about being filled with the right things.

It's a daily surrender, a choice to live open before God. It's inviting Him to purify our motives, refine our thoughts, and align our emotions with His truth. It's living without pretence, without masks—being the same person in private that we are in public.

The world says, "Follow your heart." But the Bible says, "The heart is deceitful above all things" (Jeremiah 17:9). That's why God doesn't tell us to follow our hearts. He tells us to *guard* them, to let Him *cleanse* them, to let His Spirit *lead* them.

---

[2] John Piper, "Blessed Are the Pure in Heart," Desiring God, March 2, 1986, https://www.desiringgod.org/messages/blessed-are-the-pure-in-heart.

When Jesus is forming His nature in us through His Holy Spirit, purity stops being about pressure and starts being about peace. It's not something we perform; it's something we receive. It's freedom—freedom from guilt, shame, and the constant striving to appear good enough.

Purity isn't outdated. It's the power of God's presence shaping a generation that chooses holiness over hype, devotion over distraction, and truth over trendy. It's a reminder that the greatest beauty isn't found in appearance, but in a heart that's clean before God.

Cultivating a Pure Heart

Before Jesus says, "Blessed are the pure in heart," He says in Matthew 5:7, "Blessed are the merciful, for they will be shown mercy."

There's a divine order here. **Mercy comes before purity.**

Unless we fully understand the grace and mercy of God, none of us can live with a pure heart.

Mercy is when God gives us what we don't deserve—forgiveness, freedom, and a fresh start. God withholds the punishment we deserve. Every pure life begins at the cross, where mercy triumphed over judgment.

You cannot live a pure life until you first know what it means to be forgiven. The key to purity isn't right living—it's right believing. When we understand His pure grace towards us, we begin to live a pure life for Him.

If you're struggling with pure thoughts, pure motives, or pure choices, remember this: Purity doesn't start by cleaning up your conduct on the outside. It begins by believing you've already been made clean on the inside. Jesus has paid for everyone single one of your impure thoughts past, present and future. When you look at yourself, all you'll see is your weakness, your past, and your imperfections. But when you look at Jesus, you see mercy, grace, and righteousness.

> You cannot live a pure life until you first know what it means to be forgiven.

Paul writes in Philippians 4:8 (NLT):

> Fix your thoughts on what is true, and honorable, and right, and pure, and lovely, and admirable. Think about things that are excellent and worthy of praise.

Jesus is truth. Jesus is honourable. Jesus is pure. Jesus is lovely. Jesus is worthy of praise!

As we fix our minds on God's truth, we replace the enemy's lies. The moment you start to believe what God says about you, purity begins to flow naturally. No matter your past, your mistakes, or your baggage, through Christ you can declare:

- I am forgiven.

- I am clean.

- I am pure.

- I am righteous.

- I am a new creation.

- I am whole.

Now that's excellent and worthy of praise!

The starting point for purity: You are known by Him, and you are loved by Him.

Security in Him leads to purity in us.

Beating that addiction doesn't begin with self-discipline or self-help; it begins by saying, "God, I'm Your child."

Transformation doesn't come through striving but through surrender—not by self-determination, but by being in the presence of His grace and mercy.

- Right thinking creates right believing.

- Right believing creates right living.

- And right living flows from a heart made pure by mercy.

This is one of my favourite verses I say every morning to remind me of his unfailing love towards me:

> The steadfast love of the LORD never ceases; his mercies never come to an end; they are new every morning; great is your faithfulness. (Lamentations 3:22–23 ESV)

How Do We Stay on the Path to Purity?

David asks this question, which we probably have all asked at some point in our lives, especially when we were growing up:

> How can a young person stay on the path of purity? (Psalm 119:9)

David, the man after God's own heart, was battling with the purity of his own heart. He wasn't asking as someone who had it all together. He was asking as someone who knew the struggle firsthand.

He'd seen the damage that sin and compromise could do, and now he wanted to know how to stay clean, how to live differently.

Purity, David discovered, isn't a destination we arrive at; it's a path we walk. It's a choice we make every single day. Our hearts naturally drift left to themselves. They won't choose holiness; they'll choose comfort. That's why **purity requires pre-decision**—a choice made *before* the test comes, before the temptation shows up.

We can't stay pure by willpower alone. None of us can. True purity begins when we drop the act and come before God honestly.

So how do we stay on the path of purity?
The Bible gives us five practical and powerful ways:

1. Admit We Can't Change on Our Own

Proverbs 20:9 says, "Who can say, 'I have kept my heart pure; I am clean and without sin?'"

King Solomon recognised something we all need to admit: We can't stay pure by willpower alone. None of us can. True purity begins when we drop the act and come before God honestly.

Have you ever admitted to God that you can't do it yourself? Told Him where you struggle? Been real about the areas that trip you up again and again? He's not waiting to condemn you; He's waiting to help you. God meets honesty with healing. Purity begins when we stop pretending and start depending.

2. Pray for Purity

Psalm 51:10 is David's famous cry after his biggest failure:

> Create in me a pure heart, O God, and renew a steadfast spirit within me.

David has just messed up by having sex with another man's wife. He had sinned before God, but David didn't try to justify his mistakes—he went straight to God and asked for a new heart. His prayer wasn't, "God, help me try harder," but "God, make me new." That's the difference between religion and relationship. Religion is focused on us; relationship is focused on the Father.

Like David, we've all messed up. Maybe it wasn't to the magnitude of David's mistakes, but we've all got it wrong—and if I am honest, we will all keep getting it wrong from time to time. That's why we can't pray that prayer too often.

> Religion is focused on us; relationship is focused on the Father.

Every morning, ask God to keep you pure: "Lord, in my thoughts, my motives, my words, and my desires." It's not a one-time prayer; it's a daily conversation.

3. Live According to God's Word

Our third step goes back to Psalm 119:9. David asks, "How can a young person stay on the path to purity? By living according to your word."

You can't stay pure by following culture, trends, or social media. The world's definition of purity changes every week. But the Word of God never changes. It anchors us when everything around us is shifting.

Purity covers every part of our lives—thoughts, motives, money, relationships, and especially sexuality. I couldn't write a chapter on purity without talking about sex. Few things carry more power than sex to bless or to break us.

Take a look at *The Message* paraphrase of 1 Corinthians 6:16–20:

> There's more to sex than mere skin on skin. Sex is as much a spiritual mystery as physical act.

God designed sex as a gift, a covenant bond between a husband and wife in the boundaries of marriage. But when that gift is opened outside its purpose, it causes pain. God doesn't restrict us because He's cruel. He protects us because He's kind.

If you're in a dating season right now, choose purity over chemistry. As difficult as that might sound, the rewards are so much greater. I am so glad Chantel and I waited to have sex until we were married. It was probably one of the toughest decisions we made as a couple when we were dating, but I know God has honoured that decision. Sexual purity says to God, "I want Your way over my way." You're not saying no to pleasure; you're saying yes to God's plan. God's way always seems to work out better than our way.

Can I remind you—or maybe tell you for the very first time—that whatever has happened in this area of your life, God can restore, forgive, and heal. There is no mistake too great, no past too messy, and no sin too deep for His grace. Your story doesn't end with shame; it can begin again with mercy.

If you've made choices in the past that you now regret, bring them to Jesus. Let Him wash your heart clean and give you a fresh start. And don't walk the journey alone—pray about speaking with someone you trust: a spiritually strong friend, a small group leader, or a pastor. Let them walk with you, pray for you, and speak truth into your life so that you can walk in freedom.

God's plan isn't to condemn you but to restore you. The path of purity isn't about perfection—it's about healing, grace, and new beginnings.

4. Avoid Grumbling and Arguing

Philippians 2:14–15 says,

> Do everything without grumbling or arguing, so that you may become blameless and pure.

It's surprising, isn't it? grumbling doesn't seem like a purity issue, but it is. A grumbling heart reveals a lack of trust in God. When we argue and grumble, we allow spiritual pollution to fill our hearts.

As a Brit I love a good whine—we whine about anything and everything! You name it, we will complain about it. Sunny day, it's too hot! Winter's day, too cold! My wife, who is an American, continually pulls me up on it, because nobody likes being around a whiner or complainer. Paul in his letter to the Philippians challenges the church and reminds them and us that **gratitude purifies us**. A thankful spirit keeps your heart light and clear.

> When we argue and grumble, we allow spiritual pollution to fill our hearts.

5. Focus on Your Future Hope

First John 3:3 (NKJV) says,

> Everyone who has this hope in Him purifies himself, just as He is pure.

When you keep your eyes on Jesus and your hope in eternity, the temporary pleasures of this world lose their pull. Hope purifies us because it reminds us who we are and where we're going. The older I am becoming I realise our world is so broken and lost, and our true hope isn't in our present but in our future. Heaven is our eternal home—that fills my heart with hope! Heaven is pure and holy because of what's barred from it.

- No sin

- No sickness

- No sorrow

- No pain

- No death

- No darkness

- No wickedness

- No funeral homes

- No cemeteries

- No hospitals

- No orphanages

- No prisons

- No Portman Road (in-house Norwich joke, Google it)

"Set your minds on things above, not on earthly things" (Colossians 3:2).

We are not just trying to stay pure for purity's sake; we are preparing to see God. Purity gives us vision, clarity, and purpose—not just the now but for eternity.

Purity isn't a checklist we perform for God; it's the path we walk with Him. Every step is a response to His mercy, not an attempt to earn His approval.

When we stumble, He lifts us. When we drift, He draws us back. Purity is a path of grace, a journey of becoming more like Jesus day by day. And every time you choose His way over your way, heaven takes notice.

Here's the Challenge:

Before you turn the page, pause and take an honest inventory of your heart. Ask yourself: *What am I allowing in that is slowly shaping me away from God's best?* Purity doesn't begin with rules, it begins with awareness.

This week, choose one intentional step to guard your heart more carefully. It might mean removing something that dulls your sensitivity to God, creating a healthy boundary where one doesn't exist, or bringing something hidden into the light with a trusted, godly person.

Replace what you remove with what restores—time in God's Word, worship, prayer, and accountability. Remember, purity is not about perfection, but direction. Each decision to honour God softens the soil of your heart and strengthens your freedom. Let this be your commitment: *Above all else, I will guard my heart, because what I allow in today will shape who I become tomorrow.*

Question:
Holy Spirit, What Are You Saying to Me?

As we close this chapter on purity, take a moment to reflect: God isn't calling you to perfection; He's calling you to intimacy. Purity isn't about rules or performance; it's about an undivided heart that seeks Him above all else. When we let His mercy wash over us, choosing the path of holiness each day while embracing the blessings that flow from a pure heart— security, strength, and sight—we begin to see God in ways we never imagined.

God isn't calling you to perfection; He's calling you to intimacy.

The journey doesn't stop here. Each beatitude is a stepping stone, a spiritual posture that shapes our character and draws us closer to the heart of God. As we move into the next chapter, we'll explore another layer of the kingdom life—one that builds on purity and opens us to even greater freedom and blessing. Let the Holy Spirit continue to examine your heart, refine your desires, and guide your steps. Heaven is noticing, and so is your Father.

Take a moment to ask yourself: *Holy Spirit, what are You saying to me?*

Throughout the Old Testament David consistently communed with his own heart, reflecting deeply before God. We spend so much time communicating with others, but God invites us to search our own hearts.

- Are there impure motives hidden?

- Are there impure relationships influencing my thoughts or actions?

- Are there areas I've ignored where His mercy needs to wash over me?

Purity begins with admitting we need change. It continues with prayer, asking God to create and renew our hearts:

Prayer for a Pure Heart

Lord,

I receive Your mercy.
I stop striving for purity in my own strength and start seeking intimacy with You.
Remind me again of Your grace and love.
You know me, You love me, and Your mercy is enough.
Create in me a pure heart, O God, and renew a steadfast spirit within me.

In Jesus's name, amen.

CHAPTER 4

The Broken Heart

This chapter is perhaps the hardest of all to face. One thing is certain: Life is full of heartbreak. It comes in many forms: loss, betrayal, disappointment, and grief. These moments can shake us to our core, leaving us feeling helpless, questioning, and alone. Yet even in the midst of our brokenness and pain, God's Word remains a steady anchor, offering unwavering hope, healing, and restoration. His promises remind us that no wound is beyond His touch, no sorrow too deep for His comfort, and no heart too shattered for His love to make whole again.

In Luke 4:16–19 (NKJV), Jesus declares His mission:

> "The Spirit of the LORD is upon Me, because He has anointed Me to preach the gospel to the poor; He has sent Me to heal the brokenhearted, to proclaim liberty to the captives and recovery of sight to the blind, to set at liberty those who are oppressed; to proclaim the acceptable year of the LORD."

Jesus could have chosen countless passages to usher in His mission here on earth, yet He highlights His primary purpose: to heal broken hearts. In doing so, Jesus reveals the depth of His compassion and understanding of human pain. Even today, He gently whispers, "I am here to heal your broken heart."

Brokenness often comes from separation—from loved ones, from relationships, from jobs, or from dreams. It can feel unbearable, like life is out of control. The older we get, the more we understand that life's pain is inevitable.

But even greater than the pain itself is how we choose to respond to heartbreak, for our response shapes our outcome and our future. We can walk the path of unbelief, allowing despair, bitterness, and hopelessness to take root, or we can turn toward the Comforter—the One who understands every tear, binds every wound, and leads us gently toward healing, peace, and renewed faith that transforms our sorrow into strength.

Healing is not instant like your chicken and mushroom pot noodle. Ecclesiastes 3 reminds us that there is a time to mourn, a time to heal, and a time to process. Don't rush it. God's path to healing is gentle and intentional, and it begins with prayer, surrender, and a willingness to be transformed by His presence.

The journey of healing a broken heart is not about avoiding grief or bypassing pain. It's about walking through it, letting God meet us in the depths of our sorrow, and allowing Him to transform our wounds into channels of His grace.

> God's path to healing is gentle and intentional, and it begins with prayer, surrender, and a willingness to be transformed by His presence.

Understanding Brokenness

A broken heart is not just sadness. It is extreme grief, depression, and despair that feel beyond our control. It is the inner ache of separation—whether from loved ones, dreams, security, or trust. It can feel like you're dying on inside. Some people experience this heartbreak personally; others witness it in their families or communities. But all of us will encounter it at some point.

The main cause of a broken heart is separation. Separation from relationships, from dreams, from security, from God Himself. But the good news is that Jesus specialises in mending hearts that are broken, torn, and fragmented.

Psalm 147:3 (NKJV) says: "He heals the brokenhearted and binds up their wounds."

The promise is not just for some distant future but for today. Wherever there is separation in your life, there is healing in Christ.

Two Paths in Brokenness

Every broken heart faces a choice. When tragedy strikes, we are confronted with two paths:

> Jesus specialises in mending hearts that are broken, torn, and fragmented.

1. The Path to the Comforter

This path leads to healing, hope, and restoration. It starts with complete trust in God, even when life doesn't make sense. It is a path of surrender, worship, and intimacy with Jesus. Though it is not always easy, it leads back to life.

2. The Path of Unbelief

This path leads to despair, bitterness, and emptiness. It begins when we try to navigate grief alone, questioning God's love, and refusing to surrender our need for answers. Though the pain may feel similar, the outcomes are radically different.

I've seen two believers face similar tragedies. One chose the path to the Comforter; the other, the path of unbelief. Their hearts were both broken, yet their lives took entirely different trajectories. One found peace and purpose; the other found emptiness and anger.

Every time we are facing brokenness on any level, the choice is ours.

Seven Daily Prayers for the Brokenhearted

Healing begins with conversation with God—honest, vulnerable, and heartfelt prayers that invite Him into every aspect of our pain. It is in these sacred, quiet moments of surrender that true restoration begins to take shape. As we open our hearts fully before Him, His presence brings comfort, renewal, and the gentle reminder that we are never alone. Here are seven prayers to guide your heart on the path of healing.

Prayer 1: Lord, DRAW ME close to You.

Psalm 34:18 (NLT) says, "The LORD is close to the brokenhearted; he rescues those whose spirits are crushed."

When your heart is broken, grief can feel like a vast chasm separating you from God. You may feel abandoned, lonely, or even question His presence and goodness. But what we feel and what is real are often very different. Our emotions rise and fall like the tide, but God's presence remains constant and unchanging. Even when your prayers seem to echo back in silence, He is there—listening, holding, weeping with you in the pain.

God is not afraid of our brokenness. In fact, He draws near to it. He does not turn away from our tears, frustration, or questions. God welcomes our honesty, our rawness, our confusion. He knows that true healing begins not in perfection but in surrender. When we bring Him our shattered pieces, He begins the quiet work of mending—piece by piece, breath by breath. His love is steady, not dependent on our strength or composure. He meets us right where we are, even when all we can offer Him is our pain.

God welcomes our honesty, our rawness, our confusion.

I remember a famous poem I had on my wall as a teenager called "Footprints." After my dad died, it wasn't just a poem but became my personal story.

> One night I dreamed I was walking along a beach with the Lord, scenes from my life flashing across the sky. In each scene, I noticed two sets of footprints. But during the lowest moments, only one set appeared. I asked, "Lord, why weren't You there when I needed You most?" He replied, "It was then that I carried you."

Those words have never left me. They remind me that faith is not about escaping pain but discovering God's presence within it.

He does not promise that the storm will never come, but He promises to be our shelter when it does.

Hebrews 13:5 (NKJV) assures us: "I will never leave you nor forsake you."

That promise holds true in every valley, every sleepless night, and every tear that falls unseen.

So when you pray this prayer, invite God to draw near. Picture Him sitting beside you, not distant or disappointed, but deeply compassionate. Feel His hands holding your heart—steady, strong, and tender. Let His presence quiet the chaos within and remind you that you are never alone. Even in the darkest places, His light still finds you.

Personal Prayer

Lord, draw me close to You.
When my heart feels shattered, wrap me in Your presence.
When I can't feel You, remind me that You are still near.
Carry me through the nights of silence and the days of sorrow.
Teach me to trust that Your love is enough, even when nothing makes sense.
Be my refuge, my comfort, and my peace.
Hold me close, Jesus, until my heart learns to beat with hope again.
Amen.

Prayer 2: Lord, GRIEVE WITH ME in my brokenness.

Isaiah 53:3 (NLT) says, "He was despised and rejected—a man of sorrows, acquainted with deepest grief."

Jesus knows grief. He experienced rejection, disappointment, betrayal, and loss. He knows what it is to feel the crushing weight of sorrow and the loneliness that often follows. He understands the ache of unanswered prayers and the tears that fall silently in the night.

> The ability to grieve is a reflection of being made in God's image.

The ability to grieve is a reflection of being made in God's image. God Himself grieves over the pain in our world—the suffering in war-torn nations, the innocent lives lost, the persecution of His people. He feels what we feel, and His heart breaks with ours. Lazarus's

John 11:35 tells us in the shortest verse in the Bible: "Jesus wept."

Even the strongest man who ever lived allowed Himself to weep. Jesus was deeply moved not only by Lazarus's death but by the sorrow of Mary and Martha. Grief connects us to the compassion of Christ. Sadly, we all face moments when we must attend a funeral or witness the suffering of those we love. Sometimes, that pain can touch us even more deeply than our own loss.

But grief is not weakness. When we allow ourselves to mourn, we follow the example of Christ. He doesn't merely watch from afar. He sits beside us in the ashes, holding us through every wave of sorrow.

I will never forget the day and days following my dad's death. I felt the presence of Jesus in such a real and tangible way as He grieved with me through my loss.

His Word says He will never leave me or forsake me. I have proven this true time and again.

When you pray this prayer, invite Jesus to walk with you through your sorrow, to grieve alongside you, and to comfort you in the depths of your brokenness. Allow His presence to remind you that even in your tears, you are deeply seen, fully known, and tenderly loved.

Personal Prayer

Lord, grieve with me in my brokenness.
When my heart aches beyond words, sit with me in the silence.
Help me to feel Your nearness in the moments I feel most alone.
Teach me that my tears are not wasted—they are seen by You.
Thank You for being the God who weeps, who enters my sorrow,
and who brings comfort that no human words can give.
Hold me close, Jesus, until my mourning turns to peace.
Amen.

Prayer 3: Lord, BRING ME into community.

When God brings healing to a broken heart, it rarely starts with answers. More often than not, it starts with a person.

God never meant for you to go through life on your own. From the very beginning, His design for humanity was relationship—with Him and with one another. When Adam stood alone in the garden, God said, "It is not good for man to be alone." That truth still echoes through our lives today. We were created for connection, for belonging, for community.

God gives us His church family for support. The church was never meant to be a weekly service we attend, but a people we belong to—a spiritual home where burdens are shared, tears are caught, and laughter is multiplied.

When we carry a broken heart alone, when we hold our sorrow close and shut others out, we are carrying a load we were never designed to bear. Healing comes through community—through the shared grace of others who walk with us, pray for us, and remind us that hope still exists, even when we cannot see it ourselves.

> The church was never meant to be a weekly service we attend, but a people we belong to.

Romans 12:15 (ESV) says, "Rejoice with those who rejoice, and weep with those who weep."

That's not a polite suggestion; it's a divine invitation into shared life. It's how the church becomes the tangible expression of Christ's love in a hurting world.

When my dad passed away, I learned this truth firsthand. In my grief, God didn't send explanations. He sent people.

He sent me an amazing family called the Hollingers, who opened their home to me for six weeks before and after my dad's passing, a safe place to grieve and mourn.

He sent Louise Holliday, a nurse, on the morning he died, who brought calm and care when everything felt chaotic.

He sent Sarah Elwell, a family friend, who gave me a shoulder to cry on and reminded me that it was okay to feel broken.

And He sent Trevor Pimlott, a pastor, who prayed over me when words failed.

Those faces were the face of Christ to me.

In the days when my heart felt shattered, it wasn't the lads from the park owho showed up. It was my church family. They didn't come with perfect words or quick fixes. They came with presence, prayer, and love.

I tell our church nearly all the time: "Everyone in this church community needs to be in a small group. Nobody is too busy. Nobody is too old. Nobody is too new. Because you *need* community—and community needs you."

When we allow others to walk with us, we discover that healing doesn't always happen in an instant. Sometimes it happens over cups of tea, in the quiet prayers of a friend, or through a simple hug on a Sunday morning. God uses His people to carry His comfort. And in doing so, He knits our hearts back together, piece by piece.

Personal Prayer

Lord, bring me into community.
Help me to open my heart to others, even when it feels safer to hide.
Surround me with people who will walk beside me, pray for me, and remind me that I'm not alone.
Teach me how to give and receive love within Your family—to weep with those who weep, and rejoice with those who rejoice.
Use my story to encourage someone else who is hurting, and make me a vessel of Your comfort.
Thank You for the gift of Your church—Your people, Your presence, Your healing through human hands.
Amen.

Prayer 4: Lord, GIVE ME courage to surrender my need to understand.

For much of life's pain and heartbreak, we don't—and never will—have answers. That's a huge truth to face.

There are so many moments that simply don't make sense. We pray, we believe, we hope—and yet things don't turn out the way we thought they would. And the questions that follow can be deafening: *Why did this happen? Why wasn't it different? Where were You, God?*

Most questions of heartbreak will remain unanswered this side of eternity. One day, we'll see clearly—but for now, we see in part. We walk by faith, not by full understanding.

This is the hardest prayer to pray on the path of healing:

"Not my will, but Yours be done."

We come to God not to argue, not to instruct Him, but to surrender. We come with open hands, trusting that even when we don't understand His ways, we can still trust His heart.

This is where grief can so easily turn into unbelief. When we cling to our need for answers, we risk closing our hearts to the One who holds them. It takes an enormous amount of courage to surrender our need to understand.

I've said this countless times. "God, I would have loved my dad to see his grandkids, to see our church, to see the fruit of his faith." And yet, it's often a continual surrender—not once, but again and again.

Jesus Himself prayed this in Luke 22:42: "Father, if You are willing, take this cup from me; yet not my will, but Yours be done." That prayer didn't remove His pain, but it rooted His heart in trust.

So as hard as it is, stop trying to make sense of it all. You won't find peace in the answers; you'll find it in surrender.

Personal Prayer

Lord, give me courage to surrender my need to understand.
When my heart aches for answers, teach me to trust instead.
Help me to release the "why" and hold on to You.
I choose to believe that You are still good, even when life doesn't make sense.
Not my will, but Yours be done. Amen.

Prayer 5: Lord, HELP ME draw close to Your Word.

When your heart has been broken, the next prayer is to ask God to help us stay close to the Healer through His Word. But let's be honest: When you're walking through grief, sometimes the last thing you want to do is open your Bible.

I don't like to admit being a pastor, but I've found that in seasons of deep sorrow, I often struggle to pick up God's Word. Not because I don't believe it, but because my heart feels so heavy. The pages that once brought comfort can suddenly feel distant or hard to face.

But every time I do open it, every time I press through the pain and return to His Word, I find His presence waiting for me there—stronger, deeper, and nearer than before.

The devil knows this. During seasons of loss, grief, and heartbreak, he will do everything he can to keep you from the Word of God. He whispers lies like, "It won't help," "It's too late," "Just keep scrolling and swiping," or "You're too broken." But that's exactly when you need His truth most.

Isaiah 40:29 (NLT) says, "He gives power to the weary and strength to the powerless."

Psalm 147:3 reminds us, "He heals the brokenhearted and binds up their wounds."

And Psalm 30:2 (NKJV) declares, "LORD my God, I cried out to You, and You healed me."

His Word is alive—it breathes life into lifeless hearts. It anchors us when the storm rages and gives us hope when everything feels lost.

If you ever have to visit someone who is brokenhearted, grieving, or even dying, take your Bible. You don't need clever words or polished prayers. God's Word carries power all on its own.

> His Word is alive—it breathes life into lifeless hearts.

I've stood at the bedside of many who were slipping from this world to the next, and in those moments, I often have no words of my own. But when I open Scripture and begin to read, something holy happens. They may not look at me or speak, but the moment the Word is spoken, they'll often squeeze my hand, as if their spirit recognises what their body can't respond to.

His Word gives life. Always has. Always will.

When everything else fades, His Word remains.

Personal Prayer

Lord, help me draw close to Your Word.
When grief makes it hard to open my Bible, give me strength to turn its pages anyway.
Let Your truth speak louder than my pain, and Your promises silence my fear.
When I feel weak, remind me that Your Word is life, light, and healing.
Help me to hold onto it—even when my heart is breaking—until hope rises again.
In Jesus's name, amen.

Prayer 6: Lord, in Your time USE ME to bring healing to others.

We are all in one of two places in life: Either we are walking through pain ourselves, or we are being called to comfort those who are in pain.

First Thessalonians 5:11 (NLT) reminds us: "So encourage each another and build up each other, just as you are already doing."

True followers of Christ are called to be channels of His comfort. Healing in our own lives positions us to minister to others. When we walk through heartbreak, God is shaping us into a vessel for others who are walking the same path.

I was recently watching a documentary about Hurricane Katrina. The governor of Louisiana said, "We are calling on the church to bring help and comfort." God often uses His people to meet the needs of a hurting world. That's exactly what happened the churches in Louisiana rallied and brought help and hope to that desperate community.

The first step is awareness: noticing those around you who are grieving, heartbroken, or lost. Then, being willing to step in with presence, prayer, and practical help.

Two key points for ministering to the broken hearted:

> God often uses His people to meet the needs of a hurting world.

1. Never minimise someone's pain. Avoid saying "At least . . ." or "It could be worse." Those phrases can unintentionally dismiss someone's grief. Simply being present and listening often matters more than giving advice.

2. Don't try to fix it. So often our instinct is to solve the problem immediately. While help may be needed, the first step in comfort is presence, empathy, and prayer.

God often starts the healing of a broken heart through the love and support of another person. When you pray this prayer, ask God to use you as His hands and feet—to bring comfort, encouragement, and healing to someone else, even as He continues to heal your own heart.

Personal Prayer

Lord, in Your time, use me to bring healing to others.
Take the pain I've walked through and turn it into compassion.

Open my eyes to those who are hurting, and give me the courage to reach out.
Help me to listen more than I speak, to comfort more than I correct,
and to love with the same love You've shown me.
May my scars become stories of Your faithfulness,
and may every word and act point others back to You.
In Jesus's name, amen.

Prayer 7: Lord, EXTEND TO ME purpose for my pain.

Pain has potential—when it's surrendered to God.

Left on its own, pain can make us bitter, closed, or afraid to hope again. But when placed in God's hands, pain becomes the soil where compassion, wisdom, and ministry can grow. Psychologists call this redemptive pain—the ability to transform our suffering into strength that blesses others. But long before psychology named it, Scripture declared it.

Second Corinthians 1:4 tells us:

> He comforts us in all our troubles so that we comfort others. When they are troubled, we will be able to give them the same comfort God has given us.

That verse reveals something extraordinary—your pain has purpose. What you've walked through in your loss, your brokenness isn't going to be wasted. God can take the very thing that broke you and use it to bring healing to someone else.

- Your deepest hurt can become your greatest ministry.

- A parent raising a child with special needs can offer understanding words that no one else could to others in a similair sitation.

- A survivor of addiction can walk beside someone still in the battle, speaking with empathy born of experience.

- Someone who has battled and beaten cancer can become a beacon of hope for those currently fighting the disease.

When we allow God to redeem our pain, He weaves it into His greater story. What once felt meaningless begins to carry eternal weight.

Do not judge your journey before it's over. Healing takes time, and it rarely looks how we imagined. But God is patient with our process. Every wound, every tear, every sleepless night, none of it is wasted. When we surrender it all to Him, He breathes purpose into our pain.

Think about it, the cross was the greatest symbol of suffering in history, yet God transformed it into the ultimate symbol of redemption. The same God who brought purpose from the pain of Jesus can bring purpose from yours.

Here's the Challenge:

As we close out this challenging chapter, I want to remind you that sorrow, grief, and brokenness are part of living in a fallen world. We don't get to choose the trials that come, but we do get to choose the path we walk: the path of unbelief or the path to the Comforter.

Jesus said in Luke 4:18 (NKJV), "He has sent Me to heal the brokenhearted." Friend, He can heal yours too. Healing begins when we surrender our broken heart to Him.

Today, your prayer can be simple yet powerful:

- DRAW ME

- GRIEVE WITH ME

- BRING ME

- GIVE ME

- HELP ME

- USE ME

- EXTEND TO ME

Each prayer represents a step toward intimacy with God and toward restoration of your heart. As you walk this path, you are choosing life, choosing healing, and choosing the Comforter.

Journaling Prompts

- Write a letter to God expressing your grief honestly. Don't hold back—pour out your heart.

- List three ways God has comforted you in the past. Reflect on how He might do so now.

- Identify one person you can reach out to for community or support this week.

- Journal about a past heartbreak and how God brought purpose from it.

Healing from heartbreak is a journey—it's not linear, and it takes time. But God is faithful. His Word is true: He is close to the brokenhearted, He grieves with us, He draws us into community, He gives courage to surrender, He heals, He equips us to comfort others, and He can redeem every pain for His glory.

Choose today to step onto the path of the Comforter. Let Him draw near. Let Him grieve with you. Let Him bring people alongside you. Let Him guide you in surrender, immerse you in His Word, use your pain to bless others, and give purpose to your suffering.

> Healing from heartbreak is a journey—it's not linear, and it takes time.

Question:

Holy Spirit, What Are You Saying to Me?

1. Where in my heart am I holding onto grief, sorrow, or pain?

2. Which path am I walking—the path to unbelief or the path to the Comforter?

3. Who has God placed in my life to walk alongside me during this season of brokenness?

4. How can I use my pain to comfort or encourage someone else?

5. What does surrendering my need to understand look like today?

Your broken heart is not the end of your story. In Jesus, it can become the beginning of a journey toward wholeness, hope, and healing.

When you pray this prayer, invite God to take your pain and use it. Ask Him to give you a vision for how your story—your heartbreak, your healing, your scars—can become a source of hope for others. Because when God redeems your pain, He doesn't just heal you. He uses you to heal others.

Prayer for the Brokenhearted

Lord,

Extend to me purpose for my pain.
Take what I've walked through and turn it into something that helps others find You.
Don't let my suffering be wasted—let it be transformed.

Show me who needs the comfort You've given me.
Give me courage to share my story and grace to walk beside others in theirs.
Use my life as a testimony that You bring beauty from ashes and purpose from pain.

In Jesus's name, amen.

CHAPTER 5

A Wise and Discerning Heart

When King Solomon came before the Lord at Gibeon, he was not a seasoned ruler or a man of great experience. He was young, uncertain, and overwhelmed by the weight of leadership. Many scholars believe Solomon was likely between twelve and twenty years old when he became king. Imagine that: a teenager sitting on David's throne, tasked with ruling a nation chosen by God. The people looked to him for direction, for justice, for wisdom. Yet inside, Solomon felt small, inexperienced, and deeply aware of his need for help.

In that moment, God appeared to him in a dream and said, "Ask for whatever you want me to give you" (1 Kings 3:5). What an incredible offer! The Creator of heaven and earth invites a young man to make a request with no limits. Most of us would have been tempted to ask for comfort, security, or power—a bigger army, a longer life, the defeat of enemies, or treasures beyond imagination (or maybe if you were single, a little honey?).

But Solomon's response revealed something extraordinary: "Give your servant a discerning heart to govern your people and to distinguish between right and wrong" (v. 9).

He didn't ask for what most people chase. He asked for what he needed to fulfil his calling. He recognised his weakness: "I am only a little child and do not know how to carry out my duties" (v. 7). That honesty moved the heart of God. Solomon's humility became the doorway to wisdom.

God was so pleased that He not only granted Solomon's request but also gave him what he hadn't asked for: wealth, honour, and peace (and quite a few honeys, Old Testament style). The wisdom of Solomon became legendary, but it all began with a simple prayer of dependence: "Lord, I don't know how to do this. Teach me."

Wisdom doesn't start with knowledge; it starts with surrender.

It's the awareness that we cannot lead ourselves—we need God to lead through us. Whether you're leading a nation, a family, a ministry, a football team, or simply your own heart, the same truth applies: God loves giving wisdom to those who ask.

> Wisdom doesn't start with knowledge; it starts with surrender.

James 1:5 says, "If any of you lacks wisdom, you should ask God, who gives generously to all without finding fault."

When you pray this prayer, you're not just asking for answers; you're asking for alignment with God's heart. Wisdom is not about knowing everything; it's about walking closely enough with God to sense what is right in every moment.

What Solomon was really asking for was to see his world from the perspective of God. Solomon's desire was to lead with both the mind and the heart of God.

He realised, even as a young ruler, "I can have all the power, money, and honour in the world, but unless I know what to do with them, they will eventually turn on me and destroy me." That's a truth as relevant today as it was thousands of years ago.

You can have wealth, influence, success, or fame, but unless your heart is anchored in God's wisdom, those very things can turn on you.

Without Wisdom . . .

If you ask people, "What do you want from life?" the answers are almost always the same—wealth, pleasure, success, recognition. But without the wisdom of heart, those very things will eventually turn on us.

- **Power without wisdom will turn on you.**

  Maybe you've worked under a power-hungry boss, who loved their title and position but didn't have the wisdom to handle it.

- **Money without wisdom will turn on you.**

  Why do so many lottery winners around the world end up bankrupt, addicted, or broken? Because without wisdom, money turns on you. The very thing you think will help you, hurts you.

- **Influence without wisdom will turn on you.**
  Influence is a gift, but without wisdom it becomes a weapon, often against others and eventually against yourself. When wisdom is absent, influence turns into manipulation, pride, and pressure. Instead of lifting people, it damages them. Wisdom keeps influence pure, humble, and aligned with God's purpose.

- **Knowledge without wisdom will turn on you.**
  Knowledge can fill your mind, but only wisdom can guide your heart. Without wisdom, knowledge can produce arrogance instead of understanding, Wisdom teaches us when to speak, when to listen, and how to use what we know to build rather than break.

- **Marriage without wisdom will turn on you.**
  Getting married without preparation and wisdom is like driving at seventeen without lessons, it's only a matter of time before you potentially crash.

- **Parenting without wisdom will turn on you.**
  I hear parents say, "My child is anxious, overwhelmed, struggling," and often it's because they were given too much power too soon—the power of connection, exposure, and comparison without the wisdom to handle it. A phone in a child's hand without wisdom can turn on them.

Our daughter, Miracle, has just turned fourteen and is now in high school—HELP!! As a family, we decided she doesn't need social media yet. It's not punishment; it's protection. We recognise she won't be able to handle all the pressures and rejection which social media offers, so wisdom cries out, "Wait!"

We spend years guarding our children from sharp edges, hot stoves, strangers, unsafe streets, and then one day we hand them a smartphone—one of the most powerful and potentially harmful tools ever created—and hope they'll "figure it out."

Wisdom knows when to wait.

I recently spoke to some parents who told me they spoke these words over their daughter every single day for ten years: *"You make good decisions and you hear from the Holy Spirit."* They said, "There were days she didn't make good decisions and wasn't hearing from the Holy Spirit," but they kept saying it. A decade later, that same girl is serving Jesus passionately, and her life is a testimony of the faithfulness of God and her praying parents.

> Wisdom knows when to wait.

When Solomon prayed, "Give me a discerning heart," he was asking God to shape his mind, guard his motives, and guide his leadership. And the Lord responded: "Since you have asked for wisdom and not for long life or riches, I will give you what you asked—a wise and understanding heart."

True wisdom doesn't just help you make good choices; it helps you become the kind of person God can trust with His blessings.

Here's an important truth from this passage: God will never refuse this kind of prayer.

He may not answer the prayers we pray out of comfort, comparison, or craving: "Lord, give me the latest iPhone 17," "Lord, make my life easier." Those prayers don't move heaven.

But when you start praying for the things that form your character, shape your spirit, and align you with His heart, God responds.

If you want to see instant answers to prayer, shift the focus of your prayers:

- "God, give me a wise heart."

- "God, help me to see the world as You do."

- "God, bring someone across my path today who needs encouragement."

- "God, guide my decisions and guard my motives."

These are the prayers heaven leans in to answer, because they transform you from the inside out.

Like King Solomon, this must become our daily cry:

"Lord, give me a wise and discerning heart."

When I have a wise and discerning heart, I'll know how to handle whatever I have, and I'll know how to stay faithful in what I don't have. Wisdom makes both abundance and lack meaningful.

Here's why it's important to be wise with money, because God may trust you with more, and He won't put more in your hands if those hands aren't ready.

Here's why it's important to be wise with your time, because God can multiply your hours when your priorities are His priorities.

And wisdom doesn't just guide what you do, it guides how you respond.

> Wisdom makes both abundance and lack meaningful.

Two years ago we opened our brand-new church building—it was honestly a miracle! But if this building had been completed five years earlier, it would have gone straight to my ego. Back then I was posting everything I could to grab people attention: "Look at SOUL Church! Look at me!" I wasn't ready. The platform would have been bigger than my character. So God put the dream on hold while He worked on my character.

And that's the danger: Without Christ forming us, the things we have can turn on us and destroy us.

Wisdom is God's protection over the blessings He gives.

The story of Solomon teaches us a profound truth: Wisdom is more valuable than wealth, power, or status. Solomon could have asked for anything, yet he chose to ask God for a discerning heart—a heart able to understand, judge rightly, and lead with integrity in every situation. True wisdom transforms our decisions, our relationships, and our daily lives. It is not only a spiritual gift but also a practical guide for navigating the challenges of life with clarity, humility, and purpose.

Three Biblical and Practical Ways to Gain a Heart of Wisdom

1. ASK for Wisdom

Solomon's journey toward wisdom began with one simple, yet profound action: he asked. In 1 Kings 3:9 he prays, "So give your servant a discerning heart to govern your people and to distinguish between right and wrong."

Unlike many who chase status, wealth, or influence, Solomon recognized the true need of his life: a heart and mind attuned to God's perspective. He knew he could have all the riches, honour, and power in the world, but without wisdom, those things could easily become curses rather than blessings. So he did what many never do: He asked God for the one thing that would guide everything else.

God knows far more about our lives, our world and our circumstances than we do—far beyond our experience, our education, or even our instincts.

Asking God for wisdom is not a sign of weakness; it is actually a sign of spiritual maturity. It's funny how life works, when our children are small, we are their heroes. We seem to know everything; we hold the answers to every problem. But by the time they turn thirteen, suddenly it feels like they know everything, and we know nothing! How comforting, then, to know that unlike our kids and their parents, God truly knows everything.

Asking God for wisdom is not a sign of weakness; it is actually a sign of spiritual maturity.

He sees the beginning from the end. He understands the consequences of our decisions before we even make them. And He is always ready to give wisdom generously to anyone who asks.

God does not criticize our ignorance; He does not scold us for our lack of insight. He simply gives. This is why seeking Him must become our first priority every single day.

Before breakfast, ask Him for wisdom. Before opening your laptop, your notebook, or starting your meetings, seek His counsel. The idea that we only hear from God in church, during sermons, or in special spiritual moments is a misconception.

Wisdom is available in every moment, in the ordinary routines of life, if we simply ask.

I saw this lived out in my own home. My father was a man of extraordinary spiritual wisdom in many areas. Our house in Norfolk, UK, was like a small drop-in clinic for spiritual guidance. People from all walks of life came through the door—from the local puppet man on the streets to wealthy business leaders—seeking counsel and encouragement. Even decades later, the impact remains. Recently, a man came to me and said, "Your dad gave me wisdom in my lowest point, thirty years ago." That is the enduring power of a life rooted in God's wisdom.

For pastors, leaders, parents, and anyone responsible for guiding others, asking God for wisdom is not optional; it is essential.

The decisions we make today affect the lives of many tomorrow.

As leaders, we need unprecedented wisdom in navigating complex situations in this ever-changing world, balancing truth with grace, knowing when to speak up and knowing when to shut up. So often wisdom is simply saying nothing.

Solomon's example reminds us that God delights to give wisdom when we humbly ask for it, and it is available to all who seek Him with sincerity of heart.

2. WALK with the Wise

Proverbs 13:20 (NLT) says, "Walk with the wise and become wise, associate with fools and get in trouble."

Solomon understood this principle. **A wise heart does not develop in isolation; it grows in the company of those who themselves are wise, discerning, and Christ-centred.**

When you walk with the wise, you begin to reflect their character, their thought patterns, and their way of responding to life.

Who you spend your time with will shape who you become.

I learned this early in life. Growing up, I was calm, sensible, and measured. I rarely got into trouble. My form teacher and science teacher both attend SOUL Church now, and can probably confirm that is not true! But nearly every time I did get into trouble, especially in my younger days, I wasn't alone. Someone was usually encouraging me. It was a clear pattern: When I walked with trouble, trouble walked with me. Wisdom often comes down to knowing who you allow to influence your life.

The first step out of addiction, destructive patterns, or a troubled life is disconnecting from harmful influences. A wise heart surrounds itself with other wise hearts.

If you want to change your life, sometimes you have to change your friends.

Proverbs isn't just talking about social gatherings; it's talking about the people you allow to shape your thinking, your decisions, and your spiritual posture.

I've experienced this personally in leadership and mentorship. Recently, I had lunch with the agent of a well-known sports personality in the US, a gentleman in his sixties who is also an elder in a highly respected church. I asked him, "What advice would you give to a forty-six-year-old pastor in the UK trying to build a healthy marriage, family, and church?" His response was simple, clear, and powerful—three pieces of wisdom that completely shifted my perspective:

- **Don't burn out.**
  He reminded me that creating healthy rhythms and boundaries is essential. Ministry, leadership, and life can pull us in countless directions. Without intentional rest and limits, burnout is almost inevitable. Did you know that 40 percent of pastors today are at high risk of burnout—a nearly 400 percent increase since 2015?[3] Learning to protect your heart, time, and energy is not optional; it's survival.

- **You can't want someone to change more than they do.**
  We are simply the messenger. How often do we pour energy into helping someone only to find ourselves frustrated when they aren't ready? This principle has saved me so much time, heartache, and wasted effort. It doesn't mean we stop caring or praying for others; it means we release control and focus on faithfully planting seeds, trusting God for the growth.

- **Prioritize unplugged time.**
  He said, "Whatever is happening at 8 p.m. tonight can wait until 8 a.m. tomorrow." The world is relentless, and social media, emails, and constant messages can consume our attention and distract us from what matters most. Setting boundaries, unplugging, and creating quiet space allows us to rest, think clearly, and receive wisdom from God.

All three of those nuggets of wisdom, I needed to hear, and all three I am prioritizing in my life as a result of a sixty-minute lunch.

I realized I had been walking with the wise. All three points were exactly where I was spiritually and practically. Wisdom isn't just abstract knowledge; it comes through relationships, through observation, and through listening to those who have walked the path before you. This is why small groups and mentorship relationships are vital. Wisdom is often discovered in community, in conversations, and in shared experiences.

---

[3] Barna Research (2022) quoted in "5 Shocking Realities About the Real State of Pastor Burnout," West North Carolina Conference, April 12, 2023, https://www.wnccumc.org/resourcedetail/5-shocking-realities-about-the-real-state-of-pastor-burnout-17392915.

I love clear, black-and-white wisdom from people who have lived longer, seen more, and experienced life from a broader perspective. It's a reminder that wisdom is often passed down, not discovered overnight.

They say there are three ways to learn in life:

1. From your own mistakes—costly and often painful.

2. From others' mistakes—the cheapest and safest way.

3. By not learning at all—the most expensive and regrettable path.

> Wisdom is often discovered in community, in conversations, and in shared experiences.

Parents, this principle of walking with the wise applies to raising your children too.

It's just as important to bring your kids to youth groups or to surround them with godly friends as it is to provide for their academic education.

The world bombards them with messages of self, power, and temporary success. But on Fridays, Sundays, and through intentional mentorship, we give them something eternal for their hearts. When my kids ask to spend time with like-minded Christian friends, we move everything to make that happen. This again might sound a little harsh, but we made a decision when the kids were young we won't do sleepovers at friends' houses if the parents don't share our Christian values. Not because we don't trust the families, but because we don't trust the devil.

Wisdom in relationships also applies to adults. If you want to become financially wise, walk with those who have managed money well. If you want to be happily married, walk with couples who reflect a strong, healthy marriage. When my wife and I were in Australia where we met and started to date, an amazing couple in their forties—Alan and Rosie—invited us into their home weekly. They shared wisdom, prayed with us, and invested in our lives.

Like every young couple, the first year of marriage can be a real challenge. Chantel had just moved from Los Angeles to sleepy Norfolk, and our backgrounds were very different. To be honest, we both had a lot to work through as we learned to navigate life together. I will never forget how, almost every Monday evening, Ste and Rachel—some of our good friends—invited us into their home. They cooked us a delicious meal, shared their time generously, and poured wisdom into our lives as a young married couple.

These kind of intentional relationship shapes hearts, decisions, and character. It isn't just about advice; it's about living life alongside people who have walked the path before you. Alan and Rosie, Ste and Rachel—these couples invested in us selflessly, creating safe spaces to ask questions, learn from mistakes, and grow in love and maturity.

Chantel and I are where we are today because of couples like them. Their guidance, prayers, and example taught us how to navigate disagreements, prioritize each other, and build a home centred on Christ. Wisdom, when lived out in relationships, becomes more than knowledge, it becomes a life-shaping influence that carries on for generations.

But it's not just about receiving wisdom; it's also about offering it to others. Your mistakes, your story, your struggles, and the lessons you've learned can become a guide for someone else. Often, the wisdom we've gained through pain or experience can prevent others from paying such a high price in their own lives, saving them unnecessary heartache and setbacks.

Ask yourself: Who in your world needs your time, attention, or insight? Who is walking a path you've already navigated? Maybe it's a younger colleague at work, a friend struggling in their marriage, a new parent, or a student trying to figure out life. Sharing your wisdom doesn't mean you have all the answers. It simply means you're willing to walk alongside them, speak truth in love, and model godly wisdom.

God uses ordinary lives and ordinary experiences to shape others. Your story could be the key to helping someone avoid heartache, make better choices, grow in faith, and experience hope where they thought there was none.

The Bible is clear when it says there is wisdom in a multitude of counsellors (Proverbs 15:22).

Whoever we walk with is who we are becoming.

Look at your phone: The top three people you speak to regularly tell a story about the person you are becoming. You cannot surround yourself with blindness and expect to see clearly. You cannot spend your life with defeatist, negative, or cynical people and expect to live as an overcomer.

Walking with the wise is practical, intentional, and necessary. It means making decisions about your time, your relationships, and your mentorships. It means asking, "Who is shaping my thinking today? Who am I letting speak into my heart and mind?" Solomon's wisdom wasn't just a gift; it was cultivated by his desire to surround himself with God-centred truth and guidance.

If we want to grow in wisdom, we must do the same. Seek wise friends, mentors, and communities. Prioritize their counsel. Learn from their experience. Align yourself with those who point you to God. A wise heart walks with wise hearts, and through these relationships, we learn to discern, to lead, and to live in a way that honours God and impacts the world for eternity.

3. MAKE a Decision

The third biblical way to gain a heart of wisdom is to simply make a decision. How many times are we paralyzed by the fear of making an imperfect decision? We worry about choosing the wrong path, failing, or getting it wrong. But here's a truth Solomon and Scripture teach us:

No decision is often worse than an imperfect decision.

Staying stuck, indecisive, or fearful keeps us from the growth, opportunities, and blessings God has for us.

Here's what I've discovered in life: When I make a good decision, God is with me. And when I make a bad decision, He's still with me.

Proverbs 3:5–6 (ESV) reminds us:

> Trust in the Lord with all your heart and do not lean on your own understanding. In all your ways acknowledge him, and he will make your paths straight.

This verse doesn't promise that every choice we make will be perfect. It promises that when we seek Him, He will guide our steps—even correcting and redirecting us when we get it wrong. Solomon understood that wisdom is not about avoiding mistakes; Solomon made plenty of mistakes! It's about learning to navigate life with God's guidance.

Many of us want God to hand us a clear blueprint: "Do this, not that." But God doesn't usually operate like that. He could have made us all robots, perfectly programmed to obey every instruction. But then we would accuse Him of being a control freak!

> When I make a good decision, God is with me. And when I make a bad decision, He's still with me.

The greatest gift God gave us outside of His Son, Jesus, is freedom of choice.

He doesn't force us; He gives us wisdom to decide, and He walks with us as we take each step.

God guides us in decision-making in practical ways: through His Word, through prayer, and through the counsel of wise people. If His Word says to pray, then pray. If His Word says not to do something, obey. If His Word says to step forward in faith, step forward. He gives us principles to navigate life, wisdom to evaluate options, and freedom to act.

I've learned this the hard way. After Bible school, I broke up with Chantel because I couldn't make a decision. Her mother even came over from the US wanting to wash my feet (that weirded me out!)—which, honestly, didn't help my indecision! I remember speaking to Ste my mentor one day, and he reminded me: "You're not marrying her mum!" (Thank the Lord.) That advice was simple, practical, and grounded—just what I needed to finally make a decision.

The formula is simple: **Ask God for wisdom, walk with the wise, and then make a decision.**

You will make mistakes, just like I did. But when your life is committed to following Jesus, even your mistakes can become lessons and stepping stones toward God's plan. Sometimes the right path will be clear; other times, you just have to go with what seems best, trusting God to guide your steps along the way.

Looking back over my life, I realised that my life has been shaped by a few big decisions: Moving to Bible college in Australia in 2001, marrying Chantel in 2006, moving to South Africa in 2008, starting SOUL Church in 2014.

Ask God for wisdom, walk with the wise, and then make a decision.

But more than these milestones, my life is built on the countless daily decisions, how I respond to challenges, whom I spend my time with, and how I steward the opportunities God gives me.

Here's the Challenge:

Before moving on, pause and consider the voices shaping your decisions today. Wisdom grows where humility lives. This week, intentionally seek God's wisdom before you act—through prayer, Scripture, and godly counsel. Ask yourself, *Is this choice forming my heart or hardening it?*

Choose one decision, big or small, where you will slow down, listen carefully, and respond wisely rather than react emotionally.

Above all else, guard your heart, because the direction of your life flows from it.

Question:
Holy Spirit, What Are You Saying to Me?

God doesn't just guide us through the big moments; He is present in every small decision, shaping our character, refining our hearts, and teaching us to walk wisely. The key is to act, sometimes imperfectly, knowing that He is faithful to guide, correct, and bless the steps we take in faith.

What is the Holy Spirit nudging you to do as you you've been reading through these pages?

Maybe it's creating some unplugged time away from the busyness of life so you can plug into the voice of the Spirit. Maybe it's time to make a decision. You have been delaying it and putting it off, but you know know it's time.

Whatever the Holy Spirit is asking you to do, the key is obedience. Trust God as you listen to His voice.

A Prayer for a Wise Heart

Heavenly Father,

Thank You for Your love, Your guidance, and the gift of wisdom. Today, I come before You acknowledging that I am young, inexperienced, and often uncertain, yet I long to live with a heart like Solomon's—discerning, humble, and aligned with Your ways.

Lord, I ask You for wisdom. Help me to see life through Your eyes, to discern right from wrong, and to make decisions that honour You. Teach me to trust Your guidance, to lean not on my own understanding, and to seek Your counsel in all I do. Let Your Word cry out to me each day, shaping my heart and mind.

Father, surround me with people of wisdom. Guide me to mentors, friends, and companions who will encourage me, correct me, and walk alongside me. Help me also to be a source of wisdom for others—to share my story, my lessons, and my experiences so that I can help guide and protect those who follow behind me.

Lord, give me courage to make decisions, even when they feel imperfect. Teach me that inaction is often costlier than risk, and that You are with me in every choice I make. Help me to act faithfully, trusting that You will guide my steps, correct my mistakes, and bless the decisions I make in alignment with Your will.

Father, may my heart be shaped by Your wisdom, my life transformed by Your guidance, and my daily choices reflect Your love. May I walk in discernment, surround myself with Your truth, and live boldly, trusting that You are faithful to guide, correct, and bless me.

Thank You, Lord, for the gift of wisdom, for Your presence, and for the freedom to choose. May my life honour You in every thought, word, and action.

In Jesus's name, amen.

CHAPTER 6

The Desires of My Heart

Do not fret because of those who are evil
or be envious of those who do wrong;
for like the grass they will soon wither,
like green plants they will soon die away.
Trust in the LORD and do good;
dwell in the land and enjoy safe pasture.
Take delight in the LORD,
and he will give you the desires of your heart. (Psalm 37:1–4)

Psalm 37, written by King David in his final years, is not a collection of theories or expectations. It's a record of a life lived, tested, and proven. What he wrote has stood the test for thousands of years. In these verses, David reflects on what he's learned about life, and the alignment of our hearts with God's plans and purposes.

Verse 4 is one I encourage you to memorize: "Take delight in the LORD, and he will give you the desires of your heart."

I memorized it during my first year at Bible school, and it has stuck with me ever since. There's something powerful about letting Scripture lodge itself in your heart. It has the power to shape how you think, pray, and live.

Perhaps you are experiencing and enjoying the desires of your heart right now. Or maybe you once did, but over time, life has diminished them, or circumstances have made you feel discouraged. Children, in particular, are wonderful at expressing the desires of their hearts. It might be something simple like a new pair of trainers, a visit to Five Guys, or that favourite holiday destination. Their honesty reminds us that desires are God-given; He places them in our hearts, not as a burden but as a reflection of His creativity and purpose.

Every one of us has desires planted by God in our hearts before we were even born.

> "Before I formed you in the womb I knew you,
> before you were born I set you apart;
> I appointed you to be a prophet to the nations." (Jeremiah 1:5)
>
> You saw me before I was born.
> Every day of my life was recorded in your book.
> Every moment was laid out
> before a single day had passed. (Psalm 139:16 NLT)

Every one of us has desires planted by God in our hearts before we were even born.

These verses remind us that God's knowledge and purpose for your life preceded even your physical birth.

But just as fire is good in a fireplace but dangerous if it spreads uncontrolled, desires can be misused, abused, or perverted.

The key is learning to align them with God's heart. As a twenty-six-year-old young man, I watched the church I grew up in burn down in front of my eyes after a dreadful arson attack. I felt a deep desire to see it rebuilt even at a young age, with no position, title, finance, or experience. That desire wasn't just personal ambition; it was a God-given longing to see restoration, hope, and life flourish. Nearly twenty years later I had the privilege to be part of God's desire to see it rise from ashes.

Even as a parent, I've wrestled with desires for my own children. Naturally, I pray for my daughter, Miracle-Joy, and my son, Justice-Murray, to marry someone well-educated, financially secure, and caring—good desires by any measure.

But the deepest desire of my heart and Chantel's heart is far more important. Our prayer is that our children will marry God-fearing partners. Wealth, education, and status are important, but they are secondary to our deepest desire. True joy is found when our desires align with God's purposes, for He alone knows what will sustain and fulfil their hearts eternally.

Often, we can read Psalm 37 and interpret it as if God is promising to give us whatever we want. Almost like a blank cheque. We turn it into something like: "Delight yourself in your desires, and He will give you whatever you want." But that's not what David wrote. We remove the most important part of the verse: *"in the* LORD. *"*

> True joy is found when our desires align with God's purposes.

The key to unlocking the desires of our heart is not found in dreaming harder or wishing stronger—it's in where we place our delight.

Not in our goals.

Not in our emotions.

Not in our plans.

But in Him first.

Right now, I want you to intentionally think about, and maybe even write down one deep desire in your heart. Something honest. Something real. Something you maybe haven't said out loud for years. Because the truth is, every single one of us carries desires. Some of them are healthy and God-given. Others might be bruised, buried, or even a little broken. But they're there.

Maybe your desire is:

- To be married, to find companionship and partnership

- To become a parent

- To be debt-free or mortgage-free

- To see your children sitting beside you in church

- To feel fulfilled in your job

- Or maybe it's as simple as this: "I just want to enjoy life again—every day simply feels the same."

The beautiful thing is this: God's heart is for you to experience the desires of your heart . . . as long as they align with His desires. Not because He's controlling, but because He knows what will truly satisfy you.

One of the clearest ways I can tell my relationship with God isn't where it should be is this: When I desire other things more than Him, something is off.

And it's the same in marriage. If my desire to be at football, or at work, or with my mates outweighs my desire to be with my wife, then my marriage needs attention. It's not that football or work or mates are wrong. The order of desire is what matters. God wants to give you the desires of your heart. But He wants to make sure He is your first desire.

If we chase desires without delighting in Him, we will always end up empty. But when we delight in Him first, something amazing happens: Our desires begin to align with His will, His timing, His plans. And suddenly, the things we long for begin to shift—or they begin to arrive.

We often focus so much on the desires of our heart that we skip the first part of the verse.

The delight is on me; the desires are on Him.

It's not about working harder or trying harder; it's about wanting Him more. And when we truly delight in the Lord, our desires don't just get fulfilled, they get transformed.

> If we chase desires without delighting in Him, we will always end up empty.

D.E.L.I.G.H.T.

Here are seven practices for delighting yourself in God, using the simple and memorable acronym D.E.L.I.G.H.T.

D – Dedicate My Entire Life to God

E – Enter His Presence with Thanksgiving

L – Love the Light of the World

I – Invest in Solitude

G – Give Him Praise

H – Hope in His Promises

T – Trust in His Timing

D – Dedicate My Entire Life to God

Salvation is not a one-time, emotional moment at an altar, or even a prayer. It's a daily dedication, a conscious decision to place your whole life, your plans, your future, your dreams, your desires—into the hands of the One who created you.

Delighting ourselves in God begins with surrender. It is saying, "Lord, I am Yours again today. Shape me, lead me, use me." When we consistently dedicate our entire lives to Him, something powerful begins to happen: God plants godly desires inside of us.

Romans 12:1–2 lays this out so clearly. Paul urges us to give God our bodies, our physical lives, our daily choices, as a living sacrifice. He calls this "worship," not just singing but offering ourselves. And as we surrender daily, God transforms our thinking, reshaping our desires from the inside out. The result? We learn to recognize and walk in His will which is good, pleasing, and perfect.

But notice the order: God reveals His desires *after* we dedicate our lives, not before. He asks for an advance yes. He says, "Commit first, then I'll show you what you're committing to." It feels risky, but it's actually the safest decision you could ever make, because God's plans are never harmful, they're always good, always pleasing, always perfectly crafted for who He made you to be.

Think about relationships. Early in our journey, I asked Chantel, "Do you feel called to dedicate your entire life to Jesus, anywhere, anytime, anything He might call us to do, or go?" She said yes before she knew the great adventures which laid ahead.

That's what God asks of us as well. Has anyone ever signed a contract before reading it? I highly recommend you don't! With God, we sign the contract before the terms are fully revealed because we trust the Author.

If we don't start here, we'll waste years circling our purpose without ever stepping into it. Dedication is not optional; it's foundational. For me, it's as simple and uncomfortable as each morning getting on my knees in my office and rededicating my life to God. Why? Because delight begins with dedication. Every desire He has for me flows from that place of surrender.

DEDICATE—because everything God wants to build in you begins here.

> Because delight begins with dedication.

E – Enter His Presence with Thanksgiving

Jesus says in Matthew 12:34 (NKJV), "Out of the abundance of the heart the mouth speaks."

Such a simple sentence, yet reveals so much.

Whatever fills my heart, whatever dominates my inner world, will eventually leak out of my mouth.

If my heart is full of pressure, bitterness, fear, frustration, or disappointment, my words will show it. If my heart is full of gratitude, trust, and joy, that'll show too.

A thankful mouth is simply the overflow of a thankful heart.

So the real question becomes: What is your heart full of today?

- Are you full of worry?

- Full of the ache of what hasn't happened yet?

- Full of fear of the unknown?

- Full of frustration about what should be happening by now?

Or are you thankFULL—full of gratitude, full of remembrance, full of God's goodness?

Because the truth is: Thankfulness changes the way we see life. It doesn't necessarily change all of our circumstances overnight, but it absolutely changes us in the middle of them. Delighting in God begins with thanking God.

Now, you can't talk about thankfulness without talking about its opposite, the C-word: complaining.

> Thankfulness changes the way we see life.

I know, none of you reading this book have ever complained?

But let's be honest: Complaining comes naturally, especially to us Brits! Turn on the radio, scroll social media, listen to people in a queue . . . sometimes it feels like the entire atmosphere is heavy with negativity. No wonder things don't get better. Complaining never has and never will build anything.

Complaining is the language of the flesh. Gratitude is the language of the Spirit.

And here's some truth I've discovered: If I can only be thankful when everything is going my way, I'm not growing. Even unbelievers can be thankful on a good day. The test of spiritual maturity is being thankful in all seasons.

One of the clearest signs my heart is drifting is when my complaints start to outweigh my gratitude.

Imagine if we flipped it. Imagine if we exchanged our complaints for gratitude. Imagine the atmosphere that would create in our homes, our workplaces, our marriages, and our church.

Thankfulness is such an attractive attribute in a person's character. Gratitude draws people closer; complaining pushes them away.

David reminds us of this in Psalm 100:4 (NLT):

> Enter his gates with thanksgiving; go into his courts with praise.

In those days, the "gates" were the outer entrance to Jerusalem, and the "courts" were the inner place of worship. David was saying: Lay your complaints down at the gate, don't carry them into God's presence. Enter the courts with thanksgiving, not with grumbling hearts.

Gratitude prepares the heart for worship, and worship prepares the heart for God's voice. Here's a challenge: Walk into church on a weekend and lay down your complaints at the gates, and enter into his courts with a grateful heart. Then on the way out, walk past your complaint pile and refuse to pick them up again, strolling into a new week free with a heart of gratitude.

Thankfulness isn't actually just a feeling; it's a spiritual practice that positions us to delight in God. And when we delight in Him, everything else begins to change.

L – Love the Light of the World

Our world is in a dark place right now. You don't need a prophet to tell you that; you just need to scroll your phone for thirty seconds. If we're honest, it can look like the kingdom of darkness is advancing, like chaos is winning, like fear is louder, and like evil has the microphone.

But let me remind you of something unshakeable: Our God sits on the throne. He is not pacing heaven searching for answers. He is not confused. Scripture tells us He neither slumbers nor sleeps. The God who watches over you has never once closed His eyes. And He is light. Pure, radiant, unchanging light.

And light is still stronger than darkness.

Our souls were not made to process some of the things we see and hear every day. I was sent a shocking video recently of the Charlie Kirk assassination, without any warning. In the same clip, people were jumping for joy, making memes, and celebrating. My soul was made for worship, for love, for truth, just like yours. Viewing this tragedy made my soul recoil. It made me feel physically sick.

And that's the point. Darkness is not overcome by more darkness. Darkness is overcome by light. And the only way to delight in God, the only way to navigate a world that seems increasingly angry, hostile and broken, is to love the light. To fix our hearts on Him, to saturate our minds with His light, rather than opinions, fear-driven media, or secular narratives that twist reality.

Light affects sight. Sight determines direction. And direction ultimately reveals your destination.

It's amazing how one small shift in perspective, one moment of clarity, one touch of God's light can change everything. We've all had that light-bulb moment where we suddenly look around and ask ourselves: *How did I end up here?*

- *How did I end up in this marriage that feels dead?*

- *How did I end up in this relationship I knew wasn't right?*

- *How did I end up in this courtroom, facing consequences I never expected?*

- *How did I end up in this carnage, this chaos, this crippling debt?*

- *How did I end up in this mental fog, this spiritual heaviness, this emotional exhaustion?*

And the answer, for many of us, is simple:

- We were walking blindly through life.

- We were taking steps without light.

- We were making choices without sight.

- We were following feelings instead of following Jesus.

Darkness always affects direction. Darkness causes confusion. Darkness makes you walk in circles. You think you're moving forward, but you keep ending up in the same patterns, the same relationships, the same habits, the same emotional cycles, the same disappointments.

When you walk in darkness long enough, you don't just lose your direction, you lose your sense of who you are.

So if you're in a dark place right now . . .

If life feels blurry . . .

If you just can't seem to find a way out . . .

If every direction feels confusing or overwhelming . . .

Hear this: You don't need a new map. You need a new light.

- One moment in God's presence can illuminate what years of striving never could.

- One verse from His Word can show you what hundreds of opinions never will.

- One whisper from the Holy Spirit can save you from a thousand wrong turns.

You don't need a new map. You need a new light.

Light changes everything.

And when you let the Light of the World shine into your darkness, your direction becomes clear, and your destination becomes hopeful again.

Jesus said it clearly in John 8:12:

> "I am the light of the world. Whoever follows me will never walk in darkness, but will have the light of life."

There has never been a more urgent time in history to take delight in His light. His Word is our lamp and our path, our refuge and our guide. In moments of darkness, turn to the light, not the shadows. Worship Him. Delight in Him. Fix your eyes on the only One whose light can never be dimmed, whose radiance penetrates every shadow, and whose presence will always prevail.

The world maybe growing darker, but His light is unchanging, unstoppable, and undefeated. And when we love the light, we walk in victory, even in our darkest moments.

1 – Invest in Daily Solitude

The pace of our modern world is relentless. There's always another task, another meeting, another notification, another social media post, another metric, another goal. The rhythm of life pushes us to chase growth, influence, and likes, and in the process, we lose the art of silence and solitude.

I am my own worst enemy. I just don't know when to stop. When I'm working I feel like I'm robbing time with family and friends, and when I'm with family and friends I feel like I'm robbing time from work. Can anyone relate?

Jesus understood this feeling. He constantly withdrew to be alone, not to escape life, not to wallow in hurt, but to pray, seek the Father, and align His heart with God's will. Jesus had this rhythm of advancing and retreating.

Mark 1:35 says:

> Very early in the morning, while it was still dark, Jesus got up, left the house and went off to a solitary place.

Notice the discipline. Notice the priority.

Jesus models to us that solitude isn't optional; it's essential.

But here's an important distinction: Solitude is not isolation.

- Solitude is intentionally getting alone with God.

- Isolation is getting alone with yourself, often wallowing, overthinking, or spiraling.

I know that when I'm discouraged, my first temptation is to retreat inward—to get alone with my thoughts instead of with God. But Jesus invites us to retreat with Him instead:

> "Come to me, all you who are weary and carry heavy burdens, and I will give you rest." (Matthew 11:28 NLT)

Solitude is a space to recalibrate, to surrender burdens, to be still before God, and to let Him speak. It might include lament—expressing our grief, sorrow, or frustration openly to God.

Often I will go for a run and pour out my heart to God over the turmoil in our world, the pain, the suffering, the injustices we see all around us. I lament before Him and trust Him at the same time. This is not weak faith, it's real faith.

> When was the last time you truly sat still, emptied your mind, and simply listened to God?

Psalm 46:10 (NLT) reminds us:

> "Be still, and know that I am God."

When was the last time you truly sat still, emptied your mind, and simply listened to God? This is where His desires begin to shape ours. This is where His clarity replaces our confusion and peace replaces our anxiety.

Solitude is the soil in which the seeds of godly desires, wisdom, and direction take root. It's a daily investment that transforms your heart, your mind, and your life.

H – Hope in His Promises

Hope is more than wishful thinking. It is a confident expectation anchored in the unchanging promises of God. The Bible contains over 6,000 promises, and each one is alive and active, speaking directly into our lives today.

Philippians 2:13 (NLT) says:

> For God is working in you, giving you the desire and the power to do what pleases him.

Notice the fullness of this promise: God gives us the desire to follow Him, but He doesn't stop there. He gives us the power to act on that desire. He provides the faith, courage, strength, wisdom, and resources to see His will fulfilled in our lives.

Your hope is not in circumstances, government, politics, or people; it is anchored in the one eternal name: JESUS.

The enemy's greatest fear is God's people will wake up to hope. Hope inspires us to action, and produces courage to continue when life feels impossible. Hope, rooted in God's promises, transforms our hearts and shapes our perspective. It allows us to rejoice in trials, trust in uncertainty, and walk boldly even when we cannot see the full path.

David says in Psalm 27:13 just after the news of losing a loved one, when everything seemed hopeless, "I remain confident of this: I will see the goodness of the Lord in the land of the living."

So let your heart remain confident in this, and let your hope rest fully in His promises.

T – Trust in His Timing

Ecclesiastes 3:11 says: "He has made everything beautiful in its time."

Timing is everything in life, yet one of the hardest lessons we learn is patience. We want things to happen now, on our schedule, and in our way. We get frustrated when doors don't open, when plans stall, or when prayers seem unanswered. We look around at others and think, *Why them and not me?* or *Why now and not earlier?*

I am more passionate than ever about building a Christian school in our city. Chantel and I see the need and we have the vision—we know the impact it could have. And yet, the process has been far slower than we hoped. So many times, we feel restless and frustrated. I even find myself getting frustrated at God. Yet in anything in life, it's not what we did at the beginning with the dream or at the end when it's accomplished. It's how we handle the middle, or what we now call "the messy middle."

So what do we do while we run in the middle? How do we delight ourselves in God in the middle of mess and delay?

1. **We trust Him.** Trust is more than a feeling; it's a choice to believe that God is at work, even when we cannot see it. God sees the bigger picture of our lives, the things we cannot comprehend, and He is gifting out every detail just perfectly.

2. **We remain faithful in the small things.** Waiting is not a pause, it's preparation. In the waiting season, invest in relationships, pray intentionally, serve faithfully, and grow spiritually. God

often uses the waiting season to shape our character, refine our priorities, and teach us lessons we would miss if everything happened instantly.

3. **We delight in His presence daily.** Worship, prayer, Scripture, and gratitude are not just for when life is easy. They are the tools that anchor our hearts in His timing. Even when circumstances are slow, we can **choose joy!**

> Waiting is not a pause, it's preparation.

4. **Remember this: God's timing is perfect.** What feels late to us is never late to Him. Delays are often divine interventions, shaping us, positioning us, and preparing us to receive something far greater than we imagined. When we trust Him, our waiting seasons become seasons of growth, hope, and delight.

God's timing is perfect. Delighting in Him means resting in His schedule, not ours. Often we want answers, breakthroughs, or desires to happen instantly, but God works on a divine timetable.

Here's a story from my own mum that illustrates this perfectly. Five years before my dad passed, he wanted to buy my mum a sapphire necklace for her birthday. They went into Norwich, and chose a stunning sapphire on a gold chain.

Five years later, in 2010 just after Dad had passed, Mum decided to wear her gift one evening before going out for dinner. While fastening the clasp, the precious stone fell off the chain and slipped down the plug hole. She caught the gold chain but lost the sapphire. Tears, prayer, and frantic searching followed, but it seemed gone forever. She even threw the box and receipt away to avoid dwelling on the loss.

Months later, something remarkable happened. She was standing by her stainless steel draining board in the kitchen and noticed something bright, picked it up, and realized it was the sapphire! She couldn't explain it, the box was gone, the receipt was gone, but God had placed it there, in His perfect timing. My mum's delight in God and her daily faithfulness made this moment possible.

Just like for my mum, there will be times in life when everything looks like the complete opposite of what God promised. If your desires come without obstacles, they may lead nowhere. But if you delight yourself in Him, stay faithful, and trust His timing, your desires will be fulfilled in ways far beyond your understanding.

Here's the Challenge:

Now, it's your turn. Let's practice delighting in God. Just as athletes practice daily, we train our hearts through prayer and devotion. Say this out loud:

"God, I will not pursue anything in this life which is not Your delight. I choose to delight myself in You above all else."

Question:
Holy Spirit, What Are You Saying to Me?

As you have been absorbing the words of this chapter, what has the Holy Spirit been speaking to you about? Often its personal, but the key thing is to respond.

Prayer for the Desire of My Heart

Father,

I dedicate my life to You and surrender my heart, mind, and actions to Your will.
I enter Your presence with thanksgiving, grateful for Your blessings in every season.
I choose to love Your light and shine it into the darkness around me.

Help me invest in solitude to hear Your voice and align my desires with Yours.
I give You praise for who You are, not just for what You do.
I place my hope fully in Your promises and trust that You are working in me.

Lord, I trust Your timing and rest in Your perfect plan, knowing You will give the desires of my heart according to Your will.

In Jesus's name, amen.

CHAPTER 7

All My Heart

I want to start this chapter by sharing something honest . . . something vulnerable . . . something from the very core of my heart. Something that has happened to me, and something that can happen to any one of us if we don't guard our hearts, above all else.

Some of you reading this book are new to faith—everything feels new, fresh, hopeful, a new life, new friends, new way of thinking. You've stepped into a beautiful adventure with Jesus. I am cheering you on!

But for many of you, you've been following Christ for many years. Ten, Twenty? Thirty? Forty? Fifty years?

Some of you have been on this journey longer than I've been alive! And that is incredible, I honour your faith journey and so does God. But longevity in faith brings its own challenges.

I found Christ when I was twelve, and I understood my decision. But if I am honest, my parents' faith carried my own faith for a number of years. This is now my thirty-fifth year walking with Jesus, and I've just celebrated twenty-five years in full-time ministry.

So let me be totally open and honest with you: Whenever you've been following Christ for a long time, certain conditions can quietly form in your heart without even realizing. Not instantly, not dramatically, but slowly, subtly, and silently. And most of the time, we don't even notice it happening. We've talked about some of these throughout the book—disappointment, exhaustion, grief, unanswered prayers, unhealed wounds, unprocessed seasons. All of these can shape the heart in ways we never intended.

But when King Solomon says to "guard your heart, for everything you do flows from it" (Proverbs 4:23), he is warning us about the two great enemies of the heart:

1. Hard-heartedness - when pain calcifies into cynicism.

2. Half-heartedness - when our love for God becomes diluted, distracted, and divided.

As followers of Christ, our goal is simple but not easy: to live with a soft heart and a whole heart.

Travel Tips from Jesus

That's exactly what Jesus was building into His disciples in Luke 10. He commissions seventy-two followers to go out and spread the good news, but before they set off, He gives them the ultimate travel advice. It's like talking to your kids before they go abroad without you for the first time. I am not looking forward to that conversation!

Travel light, don't take any money.

"Do not take a purse or bag or sandals." (Luke 10:4)

This is world-class advice for my wife and kids!

When you enter someone's home, bring peace, not conflict.

"When you enter a house, first say, 'Peace to this house.'" (v. 5)

Stay focused on the mission, don't get distracted.

"Do not move around from house to house." (v. 7)

Some of us need to heed this advice immediately. How easily we get distracted in a world bombarding us with information every moment!

And then Jesus gives one last travel tip for life which we all need to hear.

Not everyone will like you.

> "But when you enter a town and are not welcomed, go into its streets and say, 'Even the dust of your town we wipe from our feet as a warning to you.'" (vv. 10–11)

Some will reject you, so stop trying to be popular. One of my close friends, Chappers, gave me a critical piece of life advice a few years back. It's called the 25 Principle.

- 25 percent of people in life will love you

- 25 percent of people in life will like you

- 25 percent of people in life put up with you

- 25 percent of people in life don't like you

This is actually quite freeing especially if you are like me and want everyone to love or like you. The reality is they just don't, and Jesus knew this. Jesus wasn't just giving them travel tips; He was teaching them how to guard their hearts as they served Him. And if the disciples needed that advice, you and I absolutely do too.

Then right in the middle of Jesus giving travel instructions to His disciples, this beautiful moment of commissioning, clarity, and purpose unfolds and He gets interrupted.

An expert in the Law, who has clearly been ear-wigging on the edge of the conversation, suddenly stands up. Luke tells us he didn't stand to learn, he stood to test Jesus.

> "Teacher," he asked, "what must I do to inherit eternal life?" (v. 25)

And right there, in front of brand-new believers, seasoned followers, and this religious expert, Jesus gives the most important commandment in the entire Word of God:

> "Love the Lord your God with ALL your heart and with all your soul and with all your strength and with all your mind; and, love your neighbor as yourself." (v. 27, emphasis added)

Now notice this, whenever people teach on the heart, it almost always becomes about the bitter heart, the twisted heart, the resentful heart, the hard heart. But before Jesus addresses any of those conditions, before He deals with the wounds, the disappointments, or the damage . . .

He starts with this:

"Love the Lord with ALL your heart."

Jesus doesn't begin by diagnosing a hard heart. He begins by diagnosing an empty or half heart. He essentially says to the expert, in front of seventy-two disciples who are freshly commissioned, full of passion, excitement, and willing to risk everything, "Right now your heart is full. But there will come a time when that fullness will be tested and can fade. Not because of sin. Not because of rebellion. Simply because life can suck it out of you." Jesus was referring to a heart that's simply depleted.

For some of you reading this book, your heart has been beating for Jesus for decades. Faithful. Consistent. Showing up week in, week out. You've heard more sermons than you can count, some of you have genuinely listened to over 10,000 sermons, podcasts, devotionals, lectures, so our hearts can become weary.

We run a SOUL Leadership Academy (SLA) from September through July each year, and these ten months are nothing short of transformational for every student who walks through our doors. It is more than a program; it is a journey of discipleship, discovery, and deep development in God's Word. Students step into an environment intentionally crafted to stretch them, shape them, and strengthen them into the leaders God has designed them to be.

Watching our SLA students begin their first classes, the excitement, the passion, the brand-new Bibles, the fresh notepads, the matching hoodies, it gave me flashbacks to my own first day in Bible school. I was that kid. Full of fire. Full of dreams. Full of expectation as I started out.

But here's the sobering reality, maybe less than half of my group even walk with Jesus today. What happened?

Yes, some developed hard hearts. But many . . . many more . . . developed depleted hearts. Not angry. Not bitter. Not rebellious. Just empty.

Because if the devil can't harden your heart . . . he will try to deplete it.

How many times do we start a new year with vision, goals, declarations, dreams of miracles and momentum. But as the year goes on, it doesn't always work out the way we imagined.

Some prayers didn't get answered. Some dreams slowed down. Some hopes took a hit.

And without realising it, your heart has shifted. Not necessarily towards sin or anger but depletion.

So Jesus knowing where the disciples were at—knowing where *we* are at—looks at us with all His love and says:

Because if the devil can't harden your heart . . . he will try to deplete it.

"Love the Lord your God with ALL your heart . . ."

Because He knows that is where restoration begins.

Half-heartedness can also surface in seasons of transition. When we know we're leaving a job, or stepping into something new, we think, *Well, I'm out of here anyway*, so we quietly disengage. We stop giving our best. We stop seeing purpose in the present.

But God never blesses what we abandon early.

Even in our last mile, He expects faithfulness, because how we finish one season determines how we enter the next.

For me, half-heartedness even tries to slip into ministry. When I preach in my own pulpit at SOUL Church, I can think, *They've heard me hundreds of times before, it's just me—Jon. Same voice. Same stories. Same jokes, predictable three points, and a big finish!* And without realizing it, I can slip into "performance mode," giving words but not giving all my heart. That's how depletion disguises itself—it convinces us that "familiar" equals "faithful."

But God doesn't anoint familiar; He anoints surrendered.

For some, half-heartedness is just the slow fatigue of ordinary life. Every day starts to feel like the movie *Groundhog Day*—same routine, same pressures, same battles. We're going through the motions of our walk with God, but doing it from a distance.

That's how depletion disguises itself—it convinces us that "familiar" equals "faithful."

Over time, life becomes something we "get through," not something we live with purpose. We smile on the outside, polished and put together, but on the inside our hearts are quietly fading. Not one big wound, but a thousand tiny ones that slowly drain the life from us.

And this is exactly how the enemy loves to work, not always with catastrophic blows, but with small, subtle cuts. A little discouragement here. A delayed answer there, just another Sunday service, another answer to prayer for someone else. Without even noticing, our hearts become half-hearted, not rebellious, not hardened, just depleted.

And the truth is this: The devil loves a half-hearted Christian. Because he doesn't need to fight them. They pose no threat.

But imagine if, in this moment right now, we took Jesus's greatest command seriously again. What if we looked heavenward and said, "Lord, I'm done living with a half heart. I give You ALL my heart again"? That one decision could change the trajectory of your entire future.

Shifting from a Half Heart to a Whole Heart

Let's look at three spiritual truths and see how God can shift us from a half heart to a whole heart.

Remember Your Identity in God's Eyes

For years, Luke 10:27 confused me more than it helped me: "Love the Lord your God with all your heart . . ."

Especially in my teenage years, I wrestled with it constantly. I'd sit in church, hands lifted high in worship, sometimes tears streaming down my face, loving God with everything in me, and then by Wednesday I'd be messing it all up and giving in to temptations. I thought something was wrong with me. I thought I wasn't spiritual enough. I believed everyone else had figured out how to love God perfectly except me.

But then, in Bible school in 2002, I had a revelation that changed everything:

Stop trying to love God more . . . and start remembering how much you're loved.

Because the truth is this:

You cannot love God with all your heart if you do not first know how deeply His heart beats for you.

We love Him because He first loved us, not the other way around. God's love is the source, not your effort. First John 4:19 says it clearly:

We love because he first loved us.

That means your love for God isn't something you manufacture. It's something you respond to.

- Human love is reactive.
  God's love is initiating.

- Human love fluctuates.
  God's love is fixed.

- Human love is earned.
  God's love is given.

- Human love is conditioned—"If you do this for me, I'll do that for you."
  God's love is unconditional—"I love you because you're Mine."

We love Him because He first loved us, not the other way around.

For the first decade of my walk with Jesus, I was trying to give God something before I had truly received anything. I kept trying to love Him with "all my heart," but my heart wasn't full. It was striving, stressing, and constantly feeling like it didn't measure up.

The moment I started focusing on His love for me instead of my love for Him, something shifted.

- My heart softened.

- My devotion deepened.

- My worship became real.

- My relationship with God stopped being about pressure and started being about presence.

Above all else, **Do you believe God loves you unconditionally?**

That's the defining question of this whole book.

Not "Do you read your Bible every day?"

Not "Do you pray long prayers?"

Not "Have you avoided sin this week?"

Not "Were you kind to your work colleague?"

But this: *Do you believe—right now, in this moment—that God loves you with an unchanging love?* Because everything changes when you do.

Most Christians don't struggle to believe God exists. They struggle to believe God loves them.

Not in a general "God loves the world" way . . . but in a personal "God loves me" way. And yet, that's the foundation of a whole-hearted life.

Identity always comes before obedience. The Old Testament law demanded: "Love God with all your heart." But it provided no power to do it. The New Covenant declares: "You are loved. Now live from that love."

Most Christians don't struggle to believe God exists. They struggle to believe God loves them.

The law pointed to what we couldn't do. Grace points to what Christ already did.

When you know who you are—loved, chosen, accepted, forgiven—loving God stops being an obligation and becomes the natural overflow of a healed heart. Let God's love renew your depleted heart.

- If your heart feels tired . . .

- If serving feels heavy . . .

- If worship feels routine . . .

- If prayer feels like a duty . . .

- If the Bible feels dry . . .

It may not be because you've drifted from church, discipline, or focus. It may simply be this: Your heart needs to be refilled with the love of God.

- A depleted heart cannot love fully.

- A wounded heart cannot love freely.

- A distracted heart cannot love deeply.

- A condemned heart cannot love confidently.

But a loved heart? A heart that knows it is held, chosen, and cherished by God? That heart can love Him with everything.

Ask yourself today . . .

- Do I truly know how much God loves me today?

- Do I believe God loves me right now—not a better version of me, but me as I am?

- Am I living out of identity . . . or insecurity?

- Am I trying to earn God's love or receive it?

The healed heart, the whole heart—the guarded heart—begins with a loved heart.

So today, right now, before anything else . . . Choose to believe rightly about how God loves you. Let that truth be the anchor of your identity. Let it fill

> The healed heart begins with a loved heart.

the empty places, soften the hard places, and strengthen the weary places. Because your heart can only be whole when it knows it is His.

Now let's look at second spiritual truth showing how God can shift us from a half heart to a whole heart.

Recall When You First Encountered Christ

For some of you, this is all brand-new.

You're still wide-eyed at everything, worship feels electric, the Bible feels alive, and church feels like home in a way you never imagined. For others today, reading through these pages might actually be the first moment you truly encounter the love of Christ, the first time you have started to understand how much God loves you. And at the end of this book, you will have the opportunity to become a follower of Christ

But for many of us, we've been following Jesus for a very long time. And here's the challenge: The longer you follow Jesus, the easier it becomes for the power of God to feel familiar, and familiarity is one of the greatest enemies of faith.

When you've been around church for years, when you've sung hundreds of worship songs, served on teams, sat through thousands of messages, and walked through every season imaginable, the things that once moved your heart can start to feel ordinary. Not because they've lost power, but because we have lost wonder.

Here's a personal analogy: My favourite movie of all time is *Home Alone*!

I remember watching it for the first time when I was twelve years old at Taverham Middle School on our last day before Christmas break. The whole class was buzzing. Popcorn, excitement, laughter, it was magical. Then I remember watching it for the first time as an adult with my family; my kids were glued to the screen, eyes wide, laughing at every moment like it was the best thing they had ever seen. And now, every Christmas Eve, the Norman family tradition is *Home Alone*.

But let's be honest, it's never quite as good as the first time. Not because the film changed, but because I changed. Because once something becomes familiar, we stop seeing it with fresh eyes.

So what do I do each Christmas Eve?

I take myself back to the first time. I remind myself of what it felt like when everything was new, when Kevin McAllister was outsmarting Harry and Marv with paint cans, blowtorches, and Micro Machines, and I was laughing like I'd never seen anything so stupid in my life. I let myself feel that sense of wonder again, that childlike excitement, that moment when the story first captured my heart. Because the story didn't change, I did.

> Once something becomes familiar, we stop seeing it with fresh eyes.

And sometimes the only way to restore the joy is to return to where it first began.

And this is the same challenge in our walk with Christ.

When Chantel and I have faced challenges in our marriage—and trust me, every marriage has them, even pastors!—one of the things we do is take ourselves back twenty-five years, to when we first fell in love. Back to the early days, the butterflies, the excitement, the wonder of discovering each other. Why? Because remembering the beginning gives strength to the present.

It's the same with Jesus. We shouldn't abandon our first love (see Revelation 2:4).

If you've been around church a long time, you can hear words like *grace, mercy, forgiveness, redemption*, and somehow they don't hit with the force they once did. You already know the Scriptures. You can predict the sermon outline. You know what the pastor is going to say before a word is spoken.

But the person sitting next to you might be hearing all of this for the first time. They're about to discover their sins can be forgiven. They're about to discover their story isn't over. They're about to discover Jesus has been chasing them for years.

Do you remember what that felt like for you?

For me, it was Billy Graham at Wembley Stadium in 1989. I was twelve years old, soaked to the bone in pouring rain. But I remember the moment—the moment grace became real, the moment Jesus became personal, the moment I knew I needed Him. That moment still anchors me today.

So here's my challenge:

Walk through the doors of church this Sunday like the excitement, the joy, the expectation, the thrill of discovering Jesus is for the first time.

Not just another Sunday, but *the* Sunday.

Not just another worship song, but *your* song.

Not just another message, but a message that could *change your life* all over again.

Open your Bible this week like it's a fresh loaf of bread.

When Chantel brings home a warm loaf, I don't say, "No thanks, I had bread last week." No, I want more. I'm hungry again. That's how we approach the Word.

Imagine if marriages approached each day like it was their first date.

Imagine if we looked at Jesus like it was our first encounter.

Imagine if we lived each day with the wonder of the beginning.

Don't abandon your first love. Go back. Remember. Let the wonder return. Let your heart beat again.

Reaffirm in Your Heart: "I'm All-In!"

In the Bible there was an Old Testament king named Hezekiah, who lived around 720 BC. In a time when many evil kings ruled Judah, Hezekiah was different. He was upright, faithful, and wholeheartedly committed to following God. Hezekiah had countless opportunities to turn away, to compromise,

Let the wonder return.

or to seek approval and comfort elsewhere. But he didn't. He led with a heart that was fully, completely and unapologetically all-in.

Look at what Scripture says about him:

> Hezekiah . . . did what was good and right and true before the Lord his God. And in every work that he began in the service of the house of God, in the law and in the commandment, to seek his God, he did it with **ALL his heart**. So he prospered. (2 Chronicles 31:20–21 NKJV, emphasis added)

Hezekiah chose to seek God every single day of his life. And let's be honest . . . just like we all do, there would have been days he didn't feel like it. Days he was angry, frustrated, or let down, even by other believers. Days he faced opposition, doubt, or fear. But he made a decision: to go all-in. And look at what happened, the Bible says he prospered. Not because it was easy, but because he refused to quit and gave God his whole heart. In the challenging days we are living in, we need the same commitment. We need hearts that are all-in.

Think about it this way: Have you ever heard the illustration about bacon and eggs? I love bacon and eggs for breakfast, lunch, and dinner, but who made the greatest commitment: the chicken or the pig? The chicken gives a part of its life, the egg. But the pig gives everything, lays down its life. Kingdom work requires the "pig mentality." God calls us to give all of ourselves, not just a portion.

Sorry if you're a vegan and that illustration offended you!

Q: Why are vegans the best friends in the world?

A: They never have beef with you :-)

(I have the worst dad jokes!)

Proverbs 3:5 reminds us:

> Trust in the Lord with ALL your heart and lean not on your own understanding.

Going all-in is costly. The stakes are high. Your comfort, your plans, even your reputation may well be challenged. But the rewards—true, lasting, God-given blessings—are far greater than anything half-hearted effort could achieve.

There are three approaches we can have toward our walk with God:

1. **Our hearts aren't in it—life goes backwards.** When your heart isn't fully engaged, your faith, your relationships, and even your personal growth stall. You drift instead of move forward.

2. **Our hearts are half in it—life stands still.**
   You can survive like this, but you won't thrive. I call it "hypo-plastic syndrome"—life becomes limited, flat, and unfulfilling. I remember working at Burger King back in 1999. My manager told me one shift, "You have all the potential in the world, Jon, but your heart's not in it, I can't promote you and I can't fire you." So often our walk with God can be just half in, half out!
   Or as the French like to say: *"comme ci, comme ça."*

3. **Our hearts are all in it — life moves forward.**
   Hezekiah prospered because he chose to go all-in. It was a pre-decision.
   Going all-in is a choice. Not just when it feels easy. Not just when you feel motivated. All-in means every day, in every season, when life is good and when it's hard. It means showing up even when you're tired, serving even when you feel overlooked, loving even when it's costly, and trusting God even when you don't understand His plan.
   - My heart's all-in for Easter services, even though I've heard the Easter story countless times.
   - My heart's all-in at Christmas, even though I've heard the story fifty-five times—Mary has a baby, three kings bring gifts, and I'm still all-in.
   - My heart's all-in when it comes to sacrificing for the One who gave it all for me—giving time, energy, resources, and every part of my life in response to His love.

It's a conscious decision to engage fully, to commit wholeheartedly, to worship, serve, and follow Jesus with every ounce of your heart, regardless of familiarity, routine, or personal comfort. Being all-in is a posture of faith, trust, and love that says, "I'm Yours, Lord, in every season, every moment, and in every circumstance, without reservation."

Psalm 27:4–5 (emphasis added) says:

> One thing I ask from the Lord, this only do I seek: that I may dwell in the house of the Lord **all** the days of my life, to gaze on the beauty of the Lord. . . . For in the day of trouble he will keep me safe in his dwelling; he will hide me in the shelter of his sacred tent and set me high upon a rock.

Being all-in is a posture of faith, trust, and love that says, "I'm Yours, Lord."

Notice David's word: *dwell*, not just pop in at Christmas or Easter. *Dwell.* Every day. In the good times and the bad.

Here's the Challenge:

Parents, our kids are watching. Are we all-in?

- I am ALL-in for my Saviour, Jesus Christ.

- I am ALL-in for those who have yet to believe.

- I am ALL-in even when others are out.

Jesus went all-in for me. The cross was not half-hearted.

My heart is ALL-in for the cause of Jesus Christ. I choose to go all-in. And I want you to ask yourself today:

> *Am I ready to give my whole heart, not part, not most, but ALL, to the One who gave everything for me?*

Because when your heart is all-in, life moves forward, God prospers your soul, and His kingdom advances through you.

Jeremiah 29:13 (emphasis added) says,

> "You will seek me and find me when you seek me with **all** your heart."

Question:

Holy Spirit, What Are You Saying to Me?

Maybe for some of you, complacency has crept in with your relationship with the Father. Maybe faith feels familiar, your walk with God has become routine. Maybe your heart is depleted, you've leading your marriage half-heartedly, raising your children without full devotion, serving God without passion. Maybe, even without realising it, you've abandoned your first love.

But today, in this moment, you can choose differently. You can rededicate your heart to Him.

Maybe you need to be honest with a close friend with whom you can trust, pray together, journey this chapter closely as you draw nearer to God.

Now, I want to invite you to do something powerful. Don't just read these words—say this prayer out loud as an act of surrender, an expression of a heart that is truly all-in. Let your voice declare your commitment, your love, your trust in God.

When you speak it aloud, it's more than words; it's a step of faith. It's saying, "Lord, I'm all-in. My heart, my mind, my soul, my strength, I give it all to You."

So right now, wherever you are, lift your voice and pray this with me:

Prayer from the Heart

Lord Jesus,

Today I remember who I am in Your eyes, deeply loved and chosen.
I recall the first time I truly met You, and I ask You to restore that wonder and passion in my heart.
And Lord, I choose to be all-in, my heart, my mind, my soul, my strength.
Use me, lead me, and help me follow You fully, every day, in every way.

In Jesus's name, amen.

CHAPTER 8

A Tale of Two Hearts

In Mark 14, we see one of the most profound pictures of sacrifice in Scripture. Jesus goes to a gathering to enjoy good food, friendship, and final conversations with His disciples before His crucifixion. He knows what is coming. They don't. For them, it's the best of times; for Him, the worst of times.

Jesus is reclining at the table, and something extraordinary happens: "While he was in Bethany, reclining at the table in the home of Simon the Leper, a woman came with an alabaster jar of very expensive perfume, made of pure nard. She broke the jar and poured the perfume on his head" (Mark 14:3).

Take note of who Jesus chooses to spend His final hours on earth with: a leper, someone shunned, avoided, and pushed to the margins of society. In that setting of humility and compassion, Mary of Bethany enters the story. She is one of the three Marys who would later stand at the tomb and witness the resurrection. What she does next is extraordinary.

Mary pours an entire jar of pure nard over Jesus's head—perfume worth a year's wages. Scholars estimate its value today would be around £37,000. To those watching, it looked reckless, excessive, even offensive. A complete waste. But in biblical culture, perfume was not a luxury item alone; it was a sacred symbol of honour, devotion, and reverence, reserved for kings, priests, and the most distinguished guests.

Mary wasn't being impulsive; she was actually being intentional. She recognised who Jesus was and what was coming. While others saw waste, she saw worth. While others calculated value, she responded with worship. Her act was costly, public, and deeply personal—a beautiful expression of a heart fully surrendered. The reaction of the disciples and maybe all of us if we had been there that day: shock, indignation, and judgement:

> "Why this waste of perfume? It could have been sold . . . and the money given to the poor." (vv. 4–5)

Jesus's response is telling:

> "Leave her alone. Why are you bothering her? She has done a beautiful thing to me. . . . She did what she could. . . . Truly I tell you, wherever the gospel is preached throughout the world, what she has done will also be told in memory of her." (Mark 14:6, 8–9)

Here we see the tale of two hearts clearly revealed:

- Mary—a heart of generosity, extravagant love, sacrificial devotion
- The disciples—hearts of selfishness, fear, and comparison

What revealed both hearts? Giving.

If I'm honest, I identify more with the disciples than I'd like to admit. Surely Jesus's inner circle should have rejoiced at Mary's sacrifice, yet they quibbled over value and motive. They missed the beauty of what was happening because selfishness and fear had blinded them. They measured and compared, worried about fairness, and lost sight of the act of worship in front of them.

Like the disciples, we are constantly tested when it comes to letting go and being generous with our resources. All of us must ask ourselves continually: *Which has the upper hand in my life, selfishness or sacrifice?*

Sacrifice is giving up something of great value expecting nothing in return. Its enemy is self, the default posture of humanity without Christ. Selfishness is easier, more comfortable, and often disguised as wisdom or fear. We see it in small ways—criticising someone else's giving, holding back our time, talent, or treasure—and big ways, like not stepping out in faith to bless others when God calls us.

When our first child, Miracle-Joy, was learning to speak, her first word was "mama"—sadly not "dada." But her second word, and her very first possessive word, was "mine." Maybe you've experienced something similar with your own children. From our earliest years on earth, we instinctively learn how to hold on. Gripping, guarding, and claiming what we believe belongs to us comes naturally. Self-preservation doesn't need to be taught; it's wired into us. And unless it's surrendered to God, that same instinct can quietly shape our hearts as adults too.

Selfishness is natural; sacrificial living is a choice.

God doesn't tempt us, He tests us. The question is always the same: "Will you cling to 'mine' or will you trust Me?"

> Selfishness is natural; sacrificial living is a choice.

Giving is a spiritual mirror. It challenges the enemy of sacrifice—selfishness—and exposes fear, greed, and mistrust. Selfishness destroys relationships, robs joy, fills us with anxiety, and steals our sleep. It whispers lies like:

- "Why waste it on the church?"

- "Why give to others when you might need it yourself?"

- "Why bless others abroad when our nation has its own needs?"

Yet Mary's example reminds us that God sees hearts before He sees amounts. She didn't calculate the cost, fear the loss, or wait for permission. She recognised the moment and responded with courageous obedience. Her giving was not measured by logic but by love, not driven by obligation but by devotion.

Jesus calls us to live with that same posture of heart—to give sacrificially when we see a need, to trust Him fully with what we place in His hands, and to walk in obedience even when others misunderstand, criticise, or question our motives.

Every act of generosity, every step of faith, reveals the condition of our hearts. The question is not about the size of the gift but the posture of the heart. God measures the intent, the courage, and the willingness to trust Him with everything we have.

This is the challenge for us today as we read these pages, will we choose a heart of Mary—generous and sacrificial—or the heart of a disciple, cautious and self-protective?

Our hearts are tested not only with money but with time, energy, attention, and devotion. Every "mine" we hold onto is an opportunity to choose faith over fear and trust over control. When we choose sacrificially, we not only honour God, we allow Him to transform our hearts, our families, and our communities.

I have seen firsthand what sacrifice can do within a community. In 2024, we opened the doors of our brand-new church here in Norwich, UK. Naturally, it seemed impossible to raise £14.5 million, especially in the financial climate shaped by COVID and the ongoing impact of the Ukraine war. Yet something powerful happened. People chose sacrifice over fear. They gave generously, faithfully, and often quietly. They went beyond what was comfortable and trusted God with what felt impossible. And today, we stand inside a miracle building, not built by wealth but by obedience, unity, and wholehearted sacrifice.

God is drawn towards the heart of sacrifice.

Takeaways from the Story of Mary of Bethany

Let's unpack five key revelations from this story as we allow it to lovingly challenge our own hearts, and invite us to let go.

1. Our Sacrifice Is unto God

Jesus interrupts the criticism immediately:

> "Leave her alone. . . . She has done a beautiful thing to me." (Mark 14:6)

Mary's sacrifice was not a public display, not a fundraising moment, and not an emotional impulse. It was deeply personal. Her offering was aimed at Jesus alone. In that room, surrounded by opinions, calculations, and criticism, Mary had one audience, Christ.

This is where we must get our giving right. How many times do we give to show or give to tell?

When we give, we are not giving to a preacher. We are not giving to a church budget. We are not giving to a project, a building, or a campaign.

We are giving through the church to God.

That distinction changes everything. Because when God becomes the recipient, comparison disappears, pressure lifts, and worship takes its place. Giving is no longer about equal amounts, but equal sacrifice. It's not about impressing people; it's simply about honouring God.

Mary's gift was not casual. It was costly.

Scholars tell us this alabaster jar contained pure nard imported from the Himalayan Mountains—rare, precious, and often saved for funerals or once-in-a-lifetime moments. This wasn't a bottle of Kouros for men; this was her most treasured costly possession.

Many of us understand this principle in everyday life. We all have things we save for special occasions, a fragrance worn only on meaningful days, a restaurant reserved for anniversaries (KFC or Panda Express, for example), a suit or dress kept for moments that matter. Mary looked at Jesus and recognised: *This is the moment. This is the One.*

She saved her greatest sacrifice for the One she loved most.

And that's the question this story presses into our hearts. Not how much did she give, but who did she give it to. Sacrifice is never measured by monetary value alone; it's measured by love.

When our hearts are aligned, sacrifice becomes worship. It stops feeling like loss and starts feeling like honour. Mary didn't leave that room regretting what she poured out. She left knowing she had honoured Jesus with her best.

The same is true for us. Every time we give with a surrendered heart, heaven receives it as worship. God sees not the figure, but the faith behind it. He sees the trust, the obedience, and the love that motivates it.

Our sacrifice is unto God, and nothing given to Him is ever wasted.

2. Our Sacrifice Won't Always Make Sense

When Mary poured out the perfume, the room immediately filled with objection. "Why this waste?" the disciples asked. They weren't questioning her love; they were questioning her logic. Their response reveals something deeply human: When we don't understand sacrifice, we label it irresponsible.

The disciples tried to make sense of what was happening. They calculated the value, assessed the alternatives, and concluded that Mary's act was excessive. And that's exactly what the human mind does when confronted with faith.

Sacrifice and sense rarely walk hand in hand.

If we wait until sacrifice makes sense, we will never truly live by faith. The moment we step toward obedience, our minds begin negotiating. We start doing the math: *That's a day's wage, a week's wage, a month's salary.* We mentally list all the other options: a holiday, a nicer car, a safety net, a meal out, a future plan. Our minds are wired to protect, preserve, and control. But sacrifice invites us to trust, release, and surrender.

> Sacrifice and sense rarely walk hand in hand.

Every time our hearts lean toward faith, our minds push back with reason. And so we live in constant tension—faith versus fear, obedience versus comfort, sacrifice versus sense. If we're honest, most of us feel that tension right now.

One of the enemy's most effective lies is subtle, quiet, and logical: "This doesn't make sense."

- You'll hear it when you're young and trying to build a future.
- When you're newly married and watching every penny.

- When you're raising kids and feeling financial pressure.

- When you're older and thinking about security and stability.

And you'll hear it again when God invites you to give sacrificially. "This doesn't make sense."

Maybe as you read this chapter, God is already speaking to you about an opportunity for sacrifice in your own world right now. And if He is, chances are you can hear those familiar words echoing in your mind: "This doesn't make sense."

When we first announced that we were building our new church home, God spoke very clearly to Chantel and me. He encouraged us to lead the charge with our giving. Almost immediately, that same phrase went round and round in our minds: *This doesn't make sense.* The numbers didn't add up. The timing felt wrong. The responsibility felt heavy. But we knew this: We couldn't ask others to step out in faith if we weren't willing to trust God ourselves.

Leadership always goes first. Sacrifice starts at the front.

There came a moment when thinking had to stop and obedience had to begin. We reached the point where we had no choice but to respond. Not because it was comfortable, but because it was right. We let go of what felt safe, trusted God with what mattered most, and stepped forward in faith. And that act of obedience didn't just change our finances; it strengthened our faith and deepened our trust in God in ways we could never have imagined. We were no longer reliant on self but our Saviour. Faith entered our hearts like we had never experienced before. I know so many others with similar stories throughout the new build project.

> Leadership always goes first. Sacrifice starts at the front.

That's the power of sacrifice. It may not make sense, but it always positions you to see God move.

Nothing about giving really ever makes sense, and that's the point. For over twelve years, our church family has moved forward through faith, not logic. Hundreds of salvations and miracles that couldn't be manufactured. Growth that couldn't be explained. Two hundred baptisms in a year? That doesn't make sense. Fifteen thousand seats for "The Wonder," our Christmas production? That doesn't make sense. A miracle building rising in Norwich during global uncertainty? That doesn't make sense.

And yet here we are!

People now look at what God has done and ask the same questions the disciples asked: "How did this happen? How did you raise the money? How did planning permission come through?" The answer is never strategy alone; it's sacrifice fuelled by faith.

I'm so grateful to be part of a church where nothing make sense but everything makes sense. Imagine the alternative: a church where everything makes sense, but nothing moves forward. Where faith is replaced with caution and obedience is delayed by overthinking.

Sacrifice doesn't make sense, but it releases strength.

Mary didn't weaken her life by pouring out the perfume; she strengthened her devotion. The jar was emptied, but her faith was filled. What looked like loss to the disciples became legacy in the kingdom of God. Jesus Himself said her act would be remembered wherever the gospel is preached.

Here's the revelation Mary understood: Sacrifice doesn't diminish you, it enlarges you.

It stretches your faith, sharpens your trust, and positions you for what God wants to do next.

> Sacrifice doesn't diminish you, it enlarges you.

So don't be alarmed when sacrifice doesn't make sense. That's often the sign that you're standing on holy ground. Faith rarely adds up on paper, but it always adds up in eternity.

3. Our Sacrifice Is Born Out of Moments We Share with Jesus

Mary wasn't having a one-off emotional moment when she broke the alabaster jar. What we see in Bethany was the overflow of a life shaped by daily sacrifice and consistent devotion. Long before she poured out the perfume, she had already poured out her time, her energy, and her resources for the sake of Jesus and His mission.

Luke 8:1–3 tells us that as Jesus travelled from town to town preaching the good news of the kingdom, the disciples were supported by women who gave out of their own means. Mary of Bethany was among them. She walked with Jesus, served Him, and supported him quietly, faithfully, and sacrificially. Her generosity in Mark 14 wasn't impulsive. It was deeply intentional, born out of relationship.

Mary had been with Jesus.

That's why her sacrifice looked different from everyone else's. She wasn't responding to pressure or expectation. She was responding to being in Christ's presence.

The closer we are to Jesus, the more our hearts align with His.

Sacrifice stops being something we calculate and becomes something we desire. When intimacy increases, generosity follows.

I saw this principle lived out in my own home. My dad was one of the most sacrificially generous men I've ever known. His generosity wasn't driven by sermons; it flowed naturally from a life spent in closeness with Jesus. Every single day, he shared moments with Christ, and over time, that intimacy shaped his heart. He didn't give because he had to; he gave because of his love for the Father.

> The closer we are to Jesus, the more our hearts align with His.

There's a simple truth at work here: It's called the law of association—"you become like those you spend time with." The more we draw near to Jesus, the ultimate example of self-giving love, the more our hearts soften and our hands open. Generosity becomes instinctive, not forced.

So here's the invitation this week: Don't start with the sacrifice. Start with Jesus.

Be with Him. Sit in His presence. Let intimacy fuel obedience. Because when we walk closely with Christ, sacrifice becomes a joyful response, not a reluctant duty.

4. *Our Sacrifice Will Never Be Forgotten*

Jesus ends this moment with one of the most extraordinary statements in all of Scripture:

> "Truly I tell you, wherever the gospel is preached throughout the world, what she has done will also be told, in memory of her."
> (Mark 14:9)

Mary didn't come seeking applause. She didn't break the jar hoping to be noticed. She wasn't chasing influence, affirmation, or legacy. She came to worship, and yet Jesus made her sacrifice unforgettable. That's the paradox of the kingdom: When we give with pure motives, God Himself ensures it's never forgotten.

It might leave our hands, but it never leaves our lives.

Sacrificial giving, when it flows from love rather than pressure, is never wasted. It may look invisible in the moment, but heaven records every act of obedience. While people often forget what they receive, God never forgets what is given in faith.

Two thousand years later, in this tale of two hearts, Mary's name is still associated with sacrifice, devotion, and worship. Judas, on the other hand, is remembered for greed and betrayal. Both lived close to Jesus. Both heard His teaching. Both witnessed His miracles. Yet their legacies could not be more different. And that

We all get to choose the legacy our lives will leave.

reminds us of a sobering truth: We all get to choose the legacy our lives will leave.

Greed always promises security but delivers isolation but sacrifice feels costly but creates eternal impact.

What we release from our hands does not disappear; it multiplies in ways we may never fully see this side of eternity.

Chantel was visiting a precious lady in our church, ninety-five years young—also named Mary. She handed Chantel an ASDA carrier bag filled with small coins. By worldly standards, it wasn't much—roughly around £20—but the weight of it wasn't in the coins, it was in the heart behind them. This was a true sacrifice. This was faith. This was worship. That quiet act, seemingly small and unnoticed by most, was loud in heaven, and it reminded us that God honours every act of obedience, no matter how small.

Mary's sacrifice immediately reminded me of the story of the little boy in the feeding of the five thousand. He had just five loaves and two small fish, hardly enough to feed a crowd of over five thousand people. Yet when he placed what he had into Jesus's hands, God multiplied it beyond all human expectation. What seems small to us, what we might dismiss as "not enough," can become a flood of provision and blessing when surrendered to God.

The lesson is clear: In God's hands, every sacrifice goes further than we can imagine. What may seem insignificant to the world—a small donation, a few hours of service, a quiet act of kindness—can ripple into eternal impact. God sees the heart, not just the gift. He values obedience, trust, and faith above size or scale.

Both of the Mary stories remind us that God honours the heart behind the sacrifice. It may feel small. It may go unnoticed here on earth. But in heaven, it matters. It leaves a legacy. It builds faith. It multiplies in ways we will never fully see, and it becomes part of a story that touches generations, just like Mary of Bethany's act did two thousand years ago.

When God asks for a small act of faith, don't measure it by size. Measure it by heart. Place it in His hands. Watch as He turns a simple offering into something extraordinary. People may forget what you gave. They may never know the cost behind it. But God knows. He sees every quiet act, every surrendered offering, every unseen decision to trust Him. And one day, Scripture tells us, He will say, "Well done."

Mary of Bethany never imagined her story would be preached across nations and generations. Yet Jesus made her sacrifice eternal. When we give with the right heart, God does the same with our obedience. Nothing surrendered to Him is ever forgotten.

5. Our Sacrifice Comes from a Thankful Heart

Let's return to our first question: *Why would Mary be so extravagant with her gift?*

The answer is found in John 11:1–4:

> Now a man named Lazarus was sick. He was from Bethany, the village of Mary and her sister Martha. (This Mary, whose brother Lazarus now lay sick, was the same one who poured perfume on the Lord and wiped his feet with her hair.) So the sisters sent word to Jesus, "Lord, the one you love is sick." When he heard this, Jesus said, "This sickness will not end in death. No, it is for God's glory so that God's Son may be glorified through it."

Grateful hearts produce sacrificial lives.

Two months later, Mary would break the alabaster jar of perfume over Jesus's head. But before that moment, something miraculous had already occurred: Jesus raised her brother Lazarus from the dead.

Mary's act of extravagant sacrifice flowed from a heart overflowing with gratitude. She wasn't counting the cost. She wasn't worrying about loss. She simply responded to God's goodness with all she had. This is a principle that resonates with us today: Grateful hearts produce sacrificial lives.

Gratitude naturally fuels generosity, courage, and bold obedience. Every one of us has reason to be thankful. We were dead in sin, yet God made us alive. We were lost, yet He found us. We were broken, yet He restored us. When we allow that gratitude to fill our hearts, it changes how we live, how we give, and how we love.

When I struggle to give sacrificially, I remind myself of God's faithfulness in my life, in Chantel's life, in our families, and in our church. This year, our church has grown over 20 percent, altars are full every week, and lives are being transformed. These are all reasons to respond with generous hearts.

Mary's story is truly a tale of two hearts.

Here's the Challenge:

Take a moment to reflect honestly: Which heart do you see most in yourself—the heart that pours out love and surrender, or the heart that holds back, protects itself, or critiques from a distance?

This week, choose one intentional act of wholehearted devotion toward Jesus. It may be expressed through generosity, worship, service, or obedience in a small but meaningful way.

Remember, Jesus is not moved by the size of the offering, but by the posture of the heart. Above all else, guard your heart—and choose to respond to Him with love, not restraint.

Question:
Holy Spirit, What Are You Saying to Me?

Which heart will have the upper hand in your life: selfishness or sacrifice? A heart of selfishness fears loss, clings to what it has, and ultimately stagnates. A heart of sacrifice gives freely, trusts boldly, and releases God's blessing to flow. Sacrifice never leaves our lives empty; it always produces a legacy of love, faith, and transformation.

Which heart do you want to be remembered by?

A Prayer for the Sacrificial Heart

Jesus,

Thank You for giving everything for us.
Search our hearts and show us where we are holding
on too tightly.
Replace fear with faith and selfishness with generosity.

Give us hearts like Mary's,
hearts that recognise Your worth
and respond with love, trust, and obedience.

We place our lives in Your hands again today.
Use all we have for Your glory.

In Your name, amen.

CHAPTER 9

A Thankful Heart

Jesus said in Matthew 12:34 (ESV), "Out of the abundance of the heart the mouth speaks." In other words, whatever is filling my heart will eventually find its way into my words, my reactions, and my outlook on life. What's happening internally will always reveal itself externally.

That's why thankfulness is not something we manufacture with our mouths; it's something that flows from a thankful heart.

Think about that word, *ThankFULL* . . . I wonder what are our hearts are full of right now?

So often, our hearts can be full of worry and anxiety about tomorrow, finances, health, or our children. For others, our hearts are full of what isn't happening yet, or frustration over what should be happening by now.

Some hearts are full of fear, fear of current affairs, uncertainty in the world, with the constant stream of negative news.

> Gratitude reminds us not just of where we are, but of how far God has already brought us.

But here's the truth: Whatever our hearts are full of will eventually shape our words, how we see, and how we live out our lives. A thankful heart has the power to change the way you view your life. It doesn't deny reality, but it reframes it through the lens of God's faithfulness. Gratitude reminds us not just of where we are, but of how far God has already brought us.

Thankfulness is a mood-changer. Maybe you've tried everything—books, pills, seminars, counselling, scrolling—which are all good and helpful in their place. But can I prescribe something simple today? A thankful heart.

Gratitude has a way of lifting heaviness, quieting anxiety, and restoring joy like nothing else can. When we intentionally focus on what God has done and the positive aspects of our lives, our hearts begin to shift. God doesn't just want us to express gratitude. He wants to fill our hearts with it.

A heart of gratitude can truly revolutionise the way we see life. What we don't appreciate, depreciates.

When gratitude is absent, even the best gifts in our lives begin to lose their value. Relationships suffer when they are taken for granted. Marriages weaken when thankfulness fades. But when appreciation is present, everything changes. When I'm thankful for Chantel, our relationship doesn't just survive; it grows stronger. When I'm thankful for my health, life itself begins to appreciate, and I steward what I've been given with greater care.

Psalm 92:1 (NLT) reminds us, "It is good to give thanks to the LORD." Life genuinely gets better when gratitude becomes our daily posture.

With Chantel being American and our children now holding dual citizenship, Thanksgiving has become a meaningful tradition in our family. Each year, on the last Thursday of November, we pause to celebrate together, reflecting on God's goodness and faithfulness. Over time, this rhythm has extended into the life of our church as well. We've adopted Thanksgiving for our staff team, intentionally closing down and gifting them this time. It's our way of saying thank you—for their sacrifice, their commitment, and everything they carry throughout the year. It's a small gesture, but one rooted in gratitude, honour, and recognising the people who make the vision possible.

Thanksgiving in the USA is rooted in a moment of gratitude during uncertainty. In 1621, early settlers and Native Americans gathered to give thanks for survival, provision, and harvest after an incredibly difficult year. It wasn't about abundance; it was about recognising God's faithfulness in hardship. Over time, Thanksgiving became a national reminder to pause, reflect, and express gratitude for blessings often overlooked. Today, families gather around tables, share meals, and say thank you—not just for what they have but for *who* they have. At its heart, Thanksgiving calls us to slow down, remember God's goodness, and choose gratitude as a way of life.

While many celebrate Thanksgiving once a year, God invites us to live every day with thankful hearts. In the busyness of school runs, work, and university deadlines, it's easy to forget to pause and say thank You to the One who made it all possible. Even beyond faith, science confirms what Scripture has always said. Gratitude eliminates toxic emotions, improves sleep, and reduces anxiety, pain, and depression. When we practise thankfulness daily, we don't just change our mood, we transform our lives.

> When we practise thankfulness daily, we don't just change our mood, we transform our lives.

Here is a transformative truth from God's Word from my favourite book of the Bible, Philippians—one that has the power to reshape how we face anxiety, fear, and uncertainty.

Paul writes the letter to the Philippi church during a season of intense pressure. The church is wrestling with disunity, fear, and anxiety about the future. Yet what makes this letter extraordinary is not just what Paul says, but where he says it from. This is not a postcard from a beach resort like Great Yarmouth. Paul is writing from a Roman prison cell—cold, dark, rat-infested, chained to guards, uncertain if he will live or die. And yet, this letter overflows with joy.

In Philippians 4:4–7, Paul gives us a countercultural pathway to peace:

> Rejoice in the Lord always. I will say it again: Rejoice! Let your gentleness be evident to all. The Lord is near. Do not be anxious about anything, but in every situation, by prayer and petition, with thanksgiving, present your requests to God. And the peace of God, which transcends all understanding, will guard your hearts and your minds in Christ Jesus.

Notice Paul doesn't say, "Rejoice when things improve," or "Rejoice when the chains come off." He says to *rejoice in the Lord*, because joy is not rooted in circumstances but in relationship. When the Lord is near, joy is always available.

Then Paul addresses anxiety head-on. "Do not be anxious about anything . . ." That feels almost impossible, until he shows us how. He doesn't say ignore your worries; he says redirect them. Every worry becomes a prayer. Every fear a petition. And crucially, every request is wrapped with thanksgiving.

Thanksgiving is the key. Gratitude shifts our focus from what we lack to who God is and what He has already done. When we pray with thanksgiving, we are declaring trust before we see the outcome.

And the result?

"The peace of God, which transcends all understanding, will guard your hearts and your minds in Christ Jesus." Not peace we manufacture but peace God provides. A peace that stands guard over our hearts and minds like a soldier at the door. The transformative truth is this: Gratitude invites peace.

Seven Truths from Philippians about Gratitude

1. Gratitude Has to Be Expressed

"Rejoice in the Lord always. I will say it again: Rejoice!" (4:4).

I wonder how hard it was for Paul to say this verse. Maybe he had to repeat it so he could believe it himself? He's in jail! Chained! Hungry! Innocent! And yet, despite his circumstances, he chooses gratitude. He chooses joy. He chooses to express his thanks to the Lord. That's the power of gratitude: It's active, not passive. It's a declaration, not just a feeling.

I wonder if you know the power of expressed gratitude. It's not enough to feel it quietly or keep it in your head. When Chantel cooks an amazing meal, it's not enough to just eat it, enjoy it, I actually have to verbalise it. I have to say, "Thank you. That's amazing. I appreciate it." That act alone strengthens connection and keeps my heart soft.

Here's the challenge: The longer we know someone, the more likely we are to take them for granted—our spouses, our children, friends, leaders, even our relationship with Jesus. He knows we love Him, but He still wants to hear it. Your spouse knows you love them, but it's the daily act of remembrance which keeps the relationship alive. I encourage you to keep expressing your gratitude. Tell people, tell God. Don't assume it's understood.

How many times did we used to be grateful for things that now frustrate us. We used to marvel at dial-up AOL Internet; now if the Wi-Fi isn't 1GB per second, we complain. We were so desperate for a baby; God heard our prayers, but now that baby screams all night and keeps us awake. How quickly we can forget that the very miracle we were longing and believing for is what frustrates us. We used to pray for revival; now, when it happens, we get irritated because we can't even get a seat in church.

> Gratitude redirects our focus. It shifts our eyes from what's missing to what is present.

Even small acts of gratitude matter. A whispered "thank you," a written note, a prayer of thanks, these are seeds planted in hearts, both ours and others'. They nurture joy, soften relationships, and open our eyes to God's ongoing goodness.

I was complaining this week about something in our new building, and God reminded me, "This is the building you prayed for." Gratitude redirects our focus. It shifts our eyes from what's missing to what is present.

Let me encourage you right now, express your gratitude again. Pause through your day and say thank you to God, to others. Verbalise it. Let it out. Psalm 107:15 (NKJV) says, "Oh, that men would give thanks to the Lord for His goodness, and for His wonderful works to the children of men!"

David repeats this cry five times in one chapter. He drives home the point: Thankfulness can never stay silent.

God has given us 86,000 seconds every day. How many of them do we actually use to say "thank you"?

I might sound a little old school here, but as a family we say thank you to God before we eat. Not as a religious obligation but as a heart of gratitude. People sometimes stare at us in the restaurant, but that's okay. Gratitude can't stay hidden; it changes our hearts, our words, our actions, and ultimately the world around us.

2. Gratitude Is the Cure for Complaining

"Do not be anxious about anything, but in every situation . . ." (4:6).

It's hard to talk about gratitude unless we also talk about the C-word. If I'm honest, I can complain with the best of them. Travelling back from South Africa recently on a ministry, I sat next to a guy who snored the entire flight. How rude! He even pierced through my noise-cancelling headphones. I tried music, prayer, asking God for more patience; I even tried passive-aggressive sighing. Nothing worked. Complaining felt far more natural than gratitude. Then God reminded me fifteen years ago when I was desperate to travel and minister anywhere, I would have gladly sat next to a snoring grandad. What a perspective-realigning moment for the pastor!

Gratitude isn't pretending things are perfect; it's finding the good in the imperfect moments.

Paul writes these words from a prison cell. Not from the comfort of a plane with movies and snack but a jail with chains on his wrists. Limited food. No freedom. And still he says there is good to be found in every situation, if we're prepared to look for it.

Gratitude isn't pretending things are perfect; it's finding the good in the imperfect moments.

If we can only be thankful when everything is going our way, we're not growing spiritually. Anyone, even someone with little to no faith, can be thankful when life is easy.

It's impossible to have gratitude in our hearts while complaints dominate our lips. One of the quickest indicators my heart isn't healthy is when my complaints start to outweigh my thankfulness. Listen to the culture around us—radio talk shows, social media, conversations—it's a constant barrage of negativity. No wonder anxiety is rising.

What if, today, this week, we intentionally exchanged complaints for gratitude? What if instead of pointing out what's wrong, we thanked God for what's right?

I've seen this play out in our marriage. Chantel and I have been married twenty years—she's one blessed girl ;-). The hardest seasons over those twenty years were never just circumstantial; they were moments when gratitude slipped. "Just another meal." "Just another day." "Another Christmas." Yet I remember our first Christmas: We had nothing, two Bible college students in Sydney with no money and KFC for our Christmas roast, yet we were beyond happy just to be together and enjoy some chicken thighs! Gratitude was high; expectations were low.

Thankfulness is so attractive on all of us, yet complaining repels. Often, we can fall out of love because we stop doing the very things that made us fall in love in the first place. Gratitude keeps love alive.

Maybe God is saying to us, "If you start thanking Me for what you do have, I'll start working on what you don't."

3. Gratitude Turns What I Have into Enough

Paul writes four simple but powerful words: "The Lord is near" (4:5).

Think about the weight of that statement. Paul isn't writing from a place of comfort. He's in chains. He's facing death. He's isolated, misunderstood, and suffering unjustly. Yet instead of fixing his attention on what's going wrong, he anchors his heart in what is unchanging: the presence of God.

Someone needs to hear this today: The Lord is near.

- You might be reading this from a hospital bed—the Lord is near.

- You might feel forgotten, overlooked, or painfully alone—the Lord is near.

- You might be anxious about tomorrow, your finances, or your future—the Lord is near.

- You might have just been made redundant—the Lord is near.

Gratitude has a way of shifting our focus like nothing else. Paul doesn't deny his pain, but he refuses to let it dominate his perspective.

When we remember who is with us, what we lack loses its power.

I've learned this in my own life. That's why my phone screensaver is always my family, not my football club The Mighty Canaries, or a picture of my favourite landscape. No! On the toughest days, when pressure mounts and emotions run high, one glance at my family reminds me of what truly matters. Gratitude re-centres my heart and restores joy.

Paul says in Philippians 1:3 (NLT): "Every time I think of you, I give thanks to my God."

4. Gratitude Empowers Me to Pray

"Do not be anxious about anything, but in every situation, by prayer and petition . . ." (4:6).

Paul doesn't just tell us to pray, he teaches us how to pray. In the middle of chains, uncertainty, and injustice, he gives believers a blueprint: Pray in every situation, and begin with thanksgiving. That order matters. Gratitude isn't an optional extra; it's the gateway into effective prayer.

So often, when life feels overwhelming, prayer becomes difficult. It is so easy for prayer to slip down the priority list of life. The needs feel too big. The problems feel endless. Even as a pastor, there are moments when the

> Don't start with what's wrong, start with what God has already done.

weight of the world makes words hard to find. But Paul shows us the way forward: Don't start with what's wrong, start with what God has already done.

Thanksgiving shifts the atmosphere of our hearts. It reminds us of God's faithfulness in the past, which builds confidence for the present and hope for the future. Gratitude doesn't ignore the problem; it simply puts the problem in perspective.

What we meditate on, we magnify.

If we meditate on our worries, anxiety grows. If we meditate on God's goodness, faith grows. Gratitude realigns our focus and strengthens our prayers.

The Bible says, "Oh, magnify the LORD with me, and let us exalt His name together" (Psalm 34:3 NKJV).

I want to challenge you: Start every prayer with thanksgiving. Write a list of what God has done, big and small. Begin with ten things and every day add one or two. Build a thanksgiving journal and, over time, watch how prayer becomes less of a struggle and more of a joy. Gratitude will open the door to deeper, bolder, faith-filled prayer.

5. Gratitude Opens the Door of Blessing

". . . present your requests to God" (Philippians 4:6).

Paul instructs us to present our requests to God, but notice the order, thanksgiving comes first. God is not intimidated by our needs or offended by our requests. In fact, He us to share them with him as our heavenly Father.

Gratitude prepares our hearts to receive what He wants to give.

It positions us correctly, not as entitled consumers but as grateful children.

I've noticed this over the years, and I don't think it's a coincidence that the most thankful people I know also seem to live the most blessed lives. Not necessarily because they have more stuff, but because they recognise blessing when it arrives. Gratitude sharpens our spiritual eyesight. It helps us see God's hand in moments others might overlook or dismiss.

As we get older, something funny happens at Christmas: The pile of presents gets smaller. People don't know what to buy you anymore. You've probably got everything you need. But my dad was the exception. He was the most grateful man I've ever known, and his pile somehow grew every year. Why? Because people love blessing grateful people. Gratitude draws generosity toward it.

The same is true in our relationship with God. A grateful heart doesn't demand; it trusts. It doesn't complain; it asks with confidence. When we come to God with a thankful heart, our requests are no longer rooted in lack or fear, but in faith and relationship.

Gratitude draws generosity toward it.

A grateful heart creates room for blessing, not because God is stingy, but because gratitude aligns us with His goodness. When we learn to say thank you before we say please, we discover that blessing isn't something we chase. It's something God delights to give.

6. Gratitude Is the Gateway to Peace

Paul finishes his thoughts with a promise that feels almost too good to be true:

> The peace of God, which transcends all understanding, will guard your hearts and your minds in Christ Jesus. (4:7)

This isn't ordinary peace. It's not the absence of trouble or the resolution of every problem. It's a supernatural peace that stands guard over your inner world when your outer world is still chaotic. Our world is desperately searching for peace right now, and people will chase it through food, drink, presents, parties, distractions, and busyness, yet Paul says peace isn't found by adding more. It's released when we become thankful for what we already have. Gratitude simplifies life. It quiets the noise. It re-centres the heart.

Maybe today your mind feels like a battlefield—anxious thoughts, racing worries, sleepless nights.

One of the most powerful, practical ways to fight for your mental health is gratitude. Paul says this peace transcends understanding, meaning it won't always make sense. You can't reason your way into it, but you can thank your way into it.

Meditate on God's love for you right now, fill your mind with what He's already done, and trust Him for what He's about to do. May gratitude become the gateway out of the pit of pain you are facing right now.

7. Gratitude Connects Me to God's Will

Paul, writing from prison later on tells the church in Thessaloniki something astonishing: "In everything give thanks; for this is the will of God in Christ Jesus for you" (1 Thessalonians 5:18 NKJV). Not *for* everything but *in* everything.

Seventy-six times in Scripture we are commanded to give thanks. That tells me gratitude isn't a personality trait; it's a spiritual discipline. Gratitude can't delegated; it's a personal responsibility, and let's be honest, when we hear this verse we think, *Paul, you've clearly never met my boss . . . seen my bank balance . . . or had dinner with my mother-in-law* (I've got a sweet one). Yet Paul wasn't writing this verse from comfort; he was writing it from the confinement of prison.

> Your circumstances don't need to shift for gratitude to begin.

Who here would love to know the perfect will of God for their life? Often we think it's hidden, mysterious, or reserved for the super-spiritual. But Paul makes it simple: Keep doing what God has already put in front of you with a thankful heart, and His plan will unfold as you go.

I've discovered this personally throughout my life: When I'm thankful, my ears are more sensitive to the voice of the Spirit. It's like gratitude tunes my heart to heaven's frequency and I make better decisions for my life and for others.

We often say subconsciously, *I'll be thankful when things change*. But Scripture flips that: Thankfulness changes things.

Your circumstances don't need to shift for gratitude to begin. Even at rock bottom, you can bless the Lord at all times. And a thankful heart just might accelerate you straight into God's perfect will.

Here's the Challenge:

So let me challenge us again: What negative thoughts do we need to replace with words of gratitude today? Where has complaining taken root when thanksgiving should be growing?

Question:
Holy Spirit, What Are You Saying to Me?

What are you thankful for in your heart that you have never fully expressed with your lips? Who in your life needs to hear, "I appreciate you. I'm grateful for you. I wouldn't be who I am without you"?

Maybe this chapter can be outworked simply by a new gratitude journal from Amazon or saying thank you to the NHS worker, our emergency services men and women, our teachers, and our incredible volunteers in our church.

Let gratitude lead your life.

A Prayer for a Thankful Heart

Holy Spirit,

Fill our hearts with gratitude today.
Help us to see Your goodness,
to thank You in every situation,
and to trust You with what's still unfolding.

Guard our hearts and minds with Your peace,
and teach us to live thankful lives.

In Jesus's name, amen.

CHAPTER 10

Freedom for the Heart

We've covered a lot of areas of the heart over the past nine chapters, but at the core of every human heart is the same longing which is freedom. Not just freedom from pressure, expectations, or circumstances of everyday life but freedom on the inside. Freedom from guilt. Freedom from shame. Freedom from habits, mindsets, and sins that keep pulling us backwards when we desperately want to move forwards.

Jesus didn't just come to make bad people good. He came to make dead hearts alive. He came to set captives free. The Bible says in John 8:36, "So if the Son sets you free, you will be free indeed." Not partially free. Not temporarily free. Free indeed!

Sin has a weight to it. Some of us feel it every day. Regret from the past. Decisions we wish we could undo. Words we can't take back. Patterns we keep repeating. For others, it's quieter hidden attitudes, bitterness, unforgiveness, pride, secret addictions, private compromises. The truth is sin always promises freedom but delivers pain.

It tells us, "This will make you happy." "You deserve this." "No one will know." Yet over time, it leaves us heavier, emptier, and further from the life God intended. And the most dangerous lie of all is this one: "You're too far gone now."

Time to counteract that lie: **You're not! Jesus came for the lost and the broken.**

Romans 3:23 says, "For all have sinned and fall short of the glory of God." Not some. Not a few. All of us.

That's why God's grace is so powerful. Grace is the unearned, unmerited, and undeserved favour of God. It simply can't be earned, only received. Jesus went to the cross carrying everything we couldn't fix ourselves.

Every sin. Every failure. Every secret. Every shame-filled moment. He took our place so our hearts can live in freedom. Letting go of sin *is the doorway to freedom* in our hearts. Freedom for the heart always begins with surrender.

So often we want Jesus to change our circumstances without touching our hearts. But real freedom comes when we let go, when we stop justifying, hiding, blaming, and managing our sin, and instead bring it into the light.

> Freedom for the heart always begins with surrender.

First John 1:9 (NKJV) says, "If we confess our sins, He is faithful and just to forgive us our sins and to cleanse us from all unrighteousness."

Notice the promise here: forgive and cleanse. A new heart means a new beginning. Salvation isn't about doing good works, joining a church, or trying harder to be better. It's about receiving a new heart.

Second Corinthians 5:17 (ESV) says, "If anyone is in Christ, he is a new creation. The old has passed away; behold, the new has come."

That means:

- Your past no longer defines you.

- Your sin no longer owns you.

- Your future is no longer hopeless.

Tim Keller said, "The great basis of Christian assurance is not how much our hearts are set on God, but how unshakably his heart is set on us."4

And today can be the day everything changes . . . you can experience true freedom for the heart. Being a Christian is not about joining a religion; it's about a relationship. A relationship which forgives you of your past, and gives you purpose for today and bright hope for tomorrow.

Here's the Challenge:

If you're ready to let go of sin, receive forgiveness, and invite Jesus to lead your life, I want to help you pray this prayer.

A Prayer of Salvation

You can pray this quietly, or out loud, right where you are:

Jesus,

I come to You just as I am. I admit that I have sinned and that I need Your forgiveness.

I believe You died on the cross for me and rose again to give me new life.

Today, I let go of my past, I turn away from my sin, and I invite You into my heart.

Be my Saviour. Be my Lord. Be the leader of my life.

Thank You for loving me, forgiving me, and setting me free.

From this day forward my heart will be free as I choose to follow You.

Amen.

Freedom Begins Today

If you prayed that prayer, heaven rejoices. Your name is written in the Book of Life. Your past is forgiven. Your heart is being made new.

Freedom for the heart isn't a destination; it's a journey that starts with one brave step. And today, you took that first step.

To help you in your journey as a believer, we encourage you to find and attend a local church where you live.

We believe that it is the heart of God for every believer to find, belong to, and grow in a community where they hear and are encouraged through the preaching and teaching of the Word. In a physical local church, you will also receive the love, guidance, and support of fellow believers and church leaders.

In the meantime, we welcome you to join us at our online church, SOUL Church UK, each Sunday where you can expect Christ-centred practical, life-giving teaching and also be a part of our online community

where you can get connected with other believers. Visit https://www.soulchurch.com/ to get started!

Above All Else . . .

Above all else, guard your heart, not just because the world is dark, but because your heart is sacred. Not because God is distant, but because He is near. Not because freedom is fragile, but because it is worth protecting.

Your heart is the wellspring of your words, your decisions, your relationships, your faith, and your future. What you allow to take root will shape the direction of your life far more than any circumstance you face.

To guard your heart is not to harden it, but to steward it wisely, choosing truth over lies, grace over guilt, surrender over striving, and faith over fear, day after day.

It is to remember that freedom for the heart is not found in perfection, performance, or pretending, but in a continual turning toward Jesus—the One who heals what is broken, restores what has been lost, and redeems what once felt beyond repair.

As you move forward from these pages , you will still face moments of temptation, disappointment, and weariness, but you will also carry something far greater: a new heart, anchored in grace and strengthened by truth. Guard it by staying close to God's Word, by living honestly before Him, by surrounding yourself with a life-giving community, and by returning often to the simplicity of the gospel—that you are loved, forgiven, and free.

Let this be your daily posture and your lifelong pursuit: to live from a heart fully surrendered to God, because when your heart is free, your life will follow. Remember: Your heart is your responsibility. I'm cheering you on!

Acknowledgements

Above all else, I give all honour, glory, and gratitude to my Lord and Saviour, Jesus Christ. This book exists because of His grace, His patience, and His unending love. Every word is written in response to His call and for His glory.

To my wife, Chantel, thank you for your unwavering support, your faith, and your constant encouragement. You carry strength, wisdom, and grace in ways that continually inspire me. I could not walk this journey without you by my side. I love you.

To my daughter, Miracle-Joy, and my son, Justice-Murray, you are daily reminders of God's goodness and faithfulness. My prayer is that your hearts will always know the love of Jesus and that you will live lives rooted in truth, courage, and purpose.

To my mum, Gillian Norman, thank you for your love, prayers, and steadfast support throughout my life. Your faith and encouragement have shaped who I am more than words can express.

To my father, Murray Norman, whose life continues to speak even in his absence—thank you for the legacy you left behind. Your influence, lessons, and love remain with me, and I honour your memory in all that I do.

To my SOUL Church family—thank you for believing, praying, serving, and walking this journey together. Your faith, generosity, and love are woven into every page of this book.

To my sister and brother-in-law, Nathan and Joy Rogers—thank you for your love, encouragement, and faithful support. Your partnership, kindness, and presence have been a constant blessing in my life.

To María José Ramírez Largo, thank you for your expertise in all the detailed steps of book production. You and editor Amanda Varian ensured everything was done with care and accuracy. Thank you as well to Stuart Smith for your creativity and professionalism in designing the book cover.

And to everyone who believed in this project, spoke life into it, prayed for it, and supported it in seen and unseen ways, thank you. This book is a testimony of what God can do when hearts are surrendered and community stands together.

All glory belongs to Him.

WHAT IF THIS IS JUST THE BEGINNING?

If reading *Above All Else* has stirred something deeper in you a hunger for more of God, a desire to live with a guarded heart, or a sense that you're called to more than comfort, then SLA may be your next step.

SOUL Leadership Academy is a fully immersive, nine-month journey designed to form hearts, strengthen faith, and activate purpose. Students from around the world are trained through hands-on ministry, foundational theology, and intentional discipleship—all rooted in the local church.

This experience also includes the opportunity to take part in SLA's annual international missions trip, serving the global Church and seeing God move beyond borders.

This is more than a course. It's a response.

SOULLEADERSHIPACADEMY.ORG